Cornwall

One of The Four Nations of Britain

An introduction to the link between Cornwall's past, present and future

Editorial Team:
W.C.H. Rowe & E.R. Nute

All rights reserved. No part of this book may be reproduced or stored mechanically or electronically without prior permission of the authors or publisher

First published in 1996
Revised Edition 2012

ISBN: 0 9529313 0 3

Published By:
Cornish Stannary Publications
© Cornish Stannary Parliament

£5.00

CONTENTS

	Page
About this Book	4
Early Contact with Classical Europe	6
The Stannaries and the Tin Trade	7
The International Business of Cornwall	9
The Censored History of Britain	10
Settle Disputes Among Yourselves	10
The Celtic Arthur	12
The National Flag	13
The White Cross Symbol of High Quality	14
9/11	14
The Foreigners of Cornwall	16
The Duchy of Cornwall	16
Mineral Rights	22
Equality Before the Law	24
The Case of Mines	25
Ownership of the Soil	26
Terra Nullus – Unclaimed Land	27
Government without Consent	29
Convene a Parliament at your Discretion	30
The Abolition of Court Profits for the Duchy	30
The Celtic Conquest of England	31
The Cornish Right to Veto English Statutes	32
Charters in International Latin	32
The Constitution of Cornwall	34
Race Relations	38
The Camelot Image	40

	Page
Anglo-Saxon Culture	43
No Victory Lasts Forever	46
An English Portrait of English Racism	48
The British	49
The Teutonic Knights	50
The Whole Duchy of Cornwall Declared Forfeit	52
Confidence in the Monarchy	53
The Balance of Power	55
Convened by a Writ of the Duke of Cornwall	57
Why a Stannary Parliament Now	59
Mining Today	62
Heirs and Successors	62
Freedom of Speech	62
Cornish University Challenge	64
Petition to the European Parliament	64
Part of Europe's Heritage	65
Cornwall Never Legally Incorporated into England	66
The trial that never was	67
Freedom to Fly the Flag	75
Cultural Diversity	76
The Camborne School of Mines	77
Minerals Plan	77
The Celtic Country of the West	78
Cornish Mining - World Heritage	79
An Gof Commemoration – 500th Anniversary	80
Cornwall and the Future	83
Conclusion	86

About This Book

The aim of this book is to enable Cornish people to learn of their heritage as the indigenous, first nation people of the island of Britain and the worldwide importance of their history and culture.

Knowing and appreciating the importance of ones origin, culture, history and language is now recognised as being of great value to the health and wellbeing of the person.

The international Human Rights articles (law) recognise this and make it illegal for persons to be assimilated into another culture or territory not of their own. (Hugh Rowe - Cornish Stannary Parliament).

<u>The Identity of the Cornish Nation</u>

<u>Nation</u>	Community of people of mainly common descent, history, language, etc forming a state or inhabiting a territory.
<u>Indigenous</u>	Originating naturally in a region.
<u>First Nation</u>	The very first people to inhabit a territory.
<u>Territory</u>	The extent of land within the jurisdiction of a ruler of a state, city etc.
<u>Duke</u>	A sovereign prince ruling a Duchy or small state.
<u>Dukedom</u>	A territory ruled by a Duke.
<u>Stannary</u>	One of the four divisions of Cornwall which combined make up the Stannaries of Cornwall, which under one jurisdiction the "Cornish Stannary Parliament" holds the irrevocable right to convene on behalf of the indigenous Cornish people, their own parliament (Charter of 1508) the parliament described in 1198 as "being of unfathomable antiquity" and thought to pre-date the Roman invasions of Britain.
<u>Kernow</u> (Cornwall)	A territory being unique in that it contains the very earliest of the indigenous, or first nation people, of the island of Britain.
<u>Identity</u>	The quality or condition of being a specified person.

The identity of the Cornish (with reference to the above long established definitions)

To be Cornish is to be of a nation. In the word Cornish the suffix "ish" is used to denote nationality as in Danish, English, Irish, Spanish, Scottish etc.

The criteria used to distinguish the indigenous Cornish as a national people in their own right are that they are the remainder of the very earliest inhabitants of the island of Britain, this recently verified by the latest genetic studies of the different peoples who form the nations of the British Isles. This genetic study "The Face of Britain" has found that "the people being most like the ancient Britons are those from Cornwall….." "Britain's Celtic and Anglo Saxon heritage varies from full Celtic ancestry in Cornwall to complete Anglo Saxon ancestry in East Anglia". This of course applies only to the indigenous Cornish and not to the whole population of Cornwall.

The nationality of being Cornish is further characterized by the fact that Cornwall had been a self-governing country with its own Kings and Earls, before becoming a dukedom (or Duchy) in 1337 and remaining constitutionally recognised as extra-territorial to the United Kingdom and continuing to retain an irrevocable chartered right to its own parliament, the Cornish Stannary Parliament, to the present day.

In conclusion

The Cornish are the direct descendants of the very first people to inhabit the island of Britain before and after the last ice age some 15,000 – 17,000 years ago. The Cornish retain their irrevocable right to self- government through their own parliament. The Cornish continue with their own ancient language, culture and customs. The Cornish being a Celtic, and not an Anglo Saxon, people and having inhabited their own territory (which is neither part of England or of the United Kingdom) for millennia, can never legitimately be described as English and therefore qualify automatically to be accepted into the European "Framework Convention for the Protection of National Minorities".

EARLY CONTACT WITH CLASSICAL EUROPE

Cornwall is the smaller of the four nations of Britain, it is located at the extreme South West of Britain. "About 440 B.C., the Greek historian Herodutus wrote of the islands called Cassiterides from which we are said to have our tin." This ancient reference to Cornwall is taken from *Tin in Social and Economic History* by E.S. Hodges, Director of the International Tin Research Council, published 1964.

Expertise in tin production, therefore, provided Cornwall with an attractive commodity as the means to communicate with the wider civilised world. Contact was made and recorded by the Greek explorer Pytheas of Massilia in 310 B.C., over twelve hundred years before the word England was ever used to describe the central part of Britain. Eighteen hundred years before Columbus, Pytheas was looking for the place where merchants from the Mediterranean had sailed north to trade their goods for tin. This trade was established long before the Greeks created a public power system of government which they called democracy.

The Greeks called the source of their precious tin the "Cassiterides", the Tin Islands, without realising that tin was only available in the far west of Britain. Pytheas referred to West Cornwall as Belerion. The location of the Cassiterides was considered to be an exclusive trade secret. Pytheas' story about his voyage to the remote tin country reveals that he considered the people to be experts in discovering and extracting tin ore and smelting it to produce the finished pure metal.

The tin people, declared Pytheas, were "civilised in their mode of life owing to their contact with foreign merchants". (*Tin in Antiquity*, by R.D. Penhallurick, The Institute of Metals, London 1986).

"I may yet proceed and infer, how super-eminently this little province of Great Britain deserves to be ranked amongst the first principles of this island, as a nation and people, whose very name, according to the ancient authority of Bochart, and the later opinion of Boerhave, is derived from Bratanack, which in the Phenician language, signifies the Land of Tin. We may incline very easily to consider our county as the parent of one general name for the whole island and that the antiquity of our tin trade has been established upon mercantile principles for at least 2400 years past". (Mineralogia Cornubiensis by William Pryce in 1774).

The spirit of Arthur, Michael Joseph and thousands of past Cornish people still lives today. Not only in the indigenous but also in the thousands of Cornish people worldwide. Indeed, a description 'Occupied Cornwall' by Taumas Colliver 1996 – an American of Cornish descent, reveals that the attempts over the past 1,000 years to absorb Cornwall into England has failed.

"References in this book to 'the English' refers only to those whose intolerance leads them to believe that they have the right to deny the culture and ways of thought of another people.

The current attempts at 'assimilation' described in this book represents a denial of the right of a people to exist. In response, these attempts are being resisted by the Cornish Stannary Parliament through representations in Europe.

Our intention is to achieve in Europe, the just and rightful position of one, if not the oldest of the nations of Europe i.e. Cornwall". (ER Nute – Cornish Stannary Parliament)

THE STANNARIES AND THE TIN TRADE

Tin is mixed with copper to produce bronze and Cornwall was therefore, of strategic importance throughout the Bronze Age. From c.500 to c.1500 with the spread of Christianity, Cornish tin was in demand for church bells throughout Europe. In modern times, tin is used as a solder and in computer hardware etc. Classical Rome used the phrase *plumbum album*, "white lead" to describe tin.

East Pool

Subsequently, the word *stannum* was incorporated into Latin as the word for tin, presumably from the Cornish language itself. The ancient Cornish Stannary seal contains the motto, *Comunitatis Stangnatorum Cornubia;* The Communities (of the) Stannaries (of) Cornwall.

The etymology *stagnum* is 'probably Celtic', according to the *Heinichen Latin-German Dictionary,* published by Teubner, Stuttgart, 1993.

The Roman connection with Cornwall, *Cornubia* in Latin, is given in the Pelican historical series which begins with Roman Britain and a reference to "leasing of the Stannaries" occurring in about 200 A.D. Leasing would indicate a negotiated agreement rather than imperial conquest from which the inevitable conclusion follows, that a political structure was in place in Cornwall by which the terms of a "lease" would be negotiated and agreed.

"I have scarcely a doubt but the Stannary Parliaments were a continuation even to our own times, of the old British courts before the times of Julius Caesar" by Rev. R. Polwhele, *The History of Cornwall* 1816.

The Times series on Roman Britain, August 1996, is typical of an Anglo-Centric view of history. Southern 'England' in 50 A.D. is mentioned without reference either to 'Britain' or the fact that the word 'England' did not come into use until about 800 A.D. The article continues:- "The high moors (around Exeter) offered little incentive to further exploration. Villages in the far west of Cornwall settled by merchants engaged in the important tin trade are thought to be of Celtic origin."

The Times would have us believe, first that the Romans had "little incentive for further exploration" beyond the moors (Exmoor and Dartmoor) and second, no interest in "the important tin trade" and even more foolishly that Cornish villages were settled by "merchants".

Is it not pure Anglo-Saxon fiction to suggest that, after the Roman Armies had crossed the Straits of Dover, Dartmoor presented a natural barrier which prevented the further expansion of the Roman Empire? Is it conceivable that English pride prevents consideration of the possibility that the Cornish had their own Celtic civilisation and were freely trading their important tin with the Phoenicians, then the Greeks and later the Romans long before the first proto-English person had set foot on this island? It appears that there was agreement leading to a situation of live and let live between Kernow and the Roman Empire as had formerly been the case with the Greeks.

Wheal Francis

It seems that the Romans were more worldly-wise than the much later English whose attempts to impose their own regulations led to withdrawal of co-operation and the loss of tin through organised smuggling by the Cornish who continued with their right to trade freely, as was their custom.

Bassett Stamps

THE INTERNATIONAL BUSINESS OF CORNWALL

Cornwall has a long and prestigious history of organised tin production for around 4000 years. The gradual establishment of an industrial and economic structure attracting international attention was the only and obvious candidate to become the guiding force in the social development of the Cornish nation.

Such an evolution in the concentration of power is recognised in most other nations as the advance of the land owning classes. The Landowners of England are still represented in the un-elected House of Lords comprising, numerically, nearly two thirds of the legislature. They have presided over a doubtful legal process that provides no equality for the culture of the indigenous Cornish.

An early Plantagenet, Richard Earl of Cornwall, purchased the title King of the Romans. This exceptional title belonged to the leader of the medieval Holy Roman Empire of central Europe. Contemporary German historians recorded that the title 'King of the Romans' was obtained by virtue of the lavish presents handed out to the right people. Although these particular presents were not the first or the last backhanders in history, our attention is focused on the source of Richard's wealth and income. We are informed that royal and religious titles were available to those who could command the vast tin deposits of Cornwall which, at that time, were the only deposits of consequence in the world. *(Schmidt Geschichte der Deutschen)*

THE CENSORED HISTORY OF BRITAIN

The information contained herein is not available through the English history curriculum which is regulated by politicians and imposed in Cornish schools by the English majority in Britain. There is regrettably little understanding of the principle of 'cultural diversity' which would permit the Cornish to decide on the content of history lessons in Cornish schools.

SETTLE DISPUTES AMONG YOURSELVES

A milestone was erected in the development from industrial power to national power when King Constantine of Kernow provided a constitutional dimension c. 700 A.D. Constantine's Edict may have been a confirmation of existing practice but it clearly proclaims:- "You seekers of tin shall settle all disputes among yourselves. Your fellows shall be your judges and arbitrators".

Even a superficial reflection upon these significant words from what is described as 'the Dark ages' by English historians, reveals an early demonstration of civilised organisation two centuries after the age of King Arthur of Camelot fame. "Arthur was known to have lived in the South West, more specifically in Kernyw (Cornwall)" *(king Arthur, King of Kings* by Jean Markale, Professor of Celtic History at the Sorbonne in Paris, Published by Gordon and Cremonesi London 1977)

Across the gulf of time we can see that, although "among yourselves" may sound simple when compared with ambiguous legalistic terminology, it is effectively an instruction to implement the home grown version of Greek democracy, perhaps with a touch of the spirit of Arthur.

The motto of the Old Cornwall Society is appropriate – *Myghtern Arthur syns yu marrow*- King Arthur is not dead.

Some suggest that the principle of "among yourselves" may have resulted from and may even have been in place at the time, of the visit to Cornwall of Pytheas of Massilia in 300 B.C., since democracy had been introduced in Greece in 600 B.C. We await more discoveries and answers to interesting questions. Perhaps the Greek merchants briought "democracy" to Cornwall or took back "among yourselves" from Cornwall and called it democracy or "people rule"? (*Demos* = the people; *krateo* – to rule, (strength)).

Incidentally, those who proclaim Westminster as 'the oldest democracy' appear to ignore the fact that the Greek word 'democracy' was first borrowed into the English language in 1536. *(The Complete Oxford English Dictionary)*

These early references establish beyond doubt the historical strength of Stannary claims to prescriptive rights at common law, while the Cornish "among yourselves" of c.700 A.D. appears to foreshadow the Norman French 'public rights' of Magna Carta of 1215 A.D. Both statements were originally written in international Latin.

Those who would describe the Westminster parliament (created by the Norman French) as the mother of parliaments, might well consider that the Cornish parliament, having been described in 1198 as 'being of unfathomable antiquity' and considered to be a Brythonic continuation from pre-Roman times, must therefore realise that the Cornish Stannary Parliament is certainly the Great Grandmother of all subsequent parliaments in Britain. **"They meet in a circle, where no man stands above another, and each can see the face of all others"** (Ancient description of the Britons). The originators of subsequent British democracy.

A further realisation might be that six hundred and fifty years ago a Cornish boy named John of Trevissa attended Glasney College at Penryn and going on to be a scholar and Don at Exeter and Queens College, Oxford, subsequently formed a compound language woven together from Germanic dialects, Norman French, Latin and the ancient British language (his own).

Since John's time, words from virtually every country on earth have been borrowed to extend this new language known as 'English'.

Having been denied knowledge of and instruction in "AGAN YETH OW HONEN" (our own language) for centuries, it should be of some little comfort to at least write, as here, in a language invented by a Cornishman.

THE CELTIC ARTHUR

King Arthur is the name given to the Celtic hero who, in around 500 A.D., halted the advance of the Anglo-Saxon invasion of Britain.

There is on record a report that riots occurred in Bodmin in 1113 A.D. when itinerant French priests rejected the Cornish belief that King Arthur was not dead. (*King Arthur King of Kings* – Jean Markale, Gordon and Cremonesi 1977)

There is no record of such riots in England where Arthur is now either dismissed as a fanciful Celtic myth or embraced as English and re-packaged in an attempt to assert racial superiority over the Celts of Britain.

So desperate have the English been to 'adopt' the Celtic Arthur as English that the Duke of Cornwall has leased Tintagel (a castle in North Cornwall associated with the Celtic Arthur) to "English" Heritage so that this state subsidised quango can present 'Arthur' to the world as if he were English. In order to accrue mystique by association, the Duke of Cornwall was also christened 'Arthur' among his forenames.

That the Cornish were described as civilised by a classical Greek in 310 B.C. and therefore more likely as candidates around 500 A.D. for the "quest of the Holy Grail" and the associated Arthurian chivalry than the barbarous Anglo-Saxons of that age, is completely ignored.

THE NATIONAL FLAG

Sir George Harrison, Keeper of the Duchy Records, author of *The Laws of the Stannaries 1829*, confirms the description 'tinners at large' to embrace anyone in any way connected with the Stannaries and their heirs and successors. Heirs and successors now includes all Cornish people.

Tamar Bridge

The origins of the Cornish flag stretch back into history. Saint Piran's white cross is known to be a very ancient design. Legend has it that tin in the shape of a white cross appeared among the black ash after the smelting process when St. Piran, the patron saint of tinners, was present. It would not have taken very long for the majority living under the symbol of the national tradition of tin manufacture, to ensure that St. Piran became the patron saint of the Cornish nation itself.

Perran Sands

The process from industrial tradition to national institution has included the flag of St. Piran, a white cross on a black background. This was originally the banner of seekers of tin but which is now internationally recognised as the national flag of Cornwall/Kernow and also "tinners at large" around the world.

THE WHITE CROSS SYMBOL OF HIGH QUALITY

The high grade of the end product has been confirmed in finds of ancient tin ingots which is indicative of a sophisticated quality control system extending to every corner of the country of Kernow. The conclusion that can be drawn is that a recognised central authority is a necessary pre-condition for the appointment of effective quality surveyors.

Detailed records are not available as to the name of the central authority. However, the name 'Stannary Parliament' is recorded in the *Oxford English Dictionary* as having first been used in the English language in 1574 under the Tudor Queen Elizabeth I. The word 'Parliament' is from the French 'to speak' and has been borrowed by both English and Cornish. Whatever the name, *Kesva* in Cornish; *Parliament* in French or *Comunitatus* in Latin, a Public Body, Grand Jury, Senate or Stannary Parliament has been in existence in some form in Cornwall at least since about 700 A.D and more likely for some 2000 years or more.

It is not generally understood that during the centuries of tin mining activity in Cornwall, the whole community was involved. Tin was the lifeblood of the Cornish nation.

The fact that tin was so prolific in Cornwall meant that virtually anyone might discover tin anywhere at any time whatever their normal trade. As a result it was for practical reasons of administration and social cohesion that the 'Stannaries' became indistinguishable from 'Cornwall and "seekers of tin" or "tinners at large", indistinguishable from 'the Cornish. The white cross became a symbol of high quality under the motto 'One and All'- Onen hag oll.

9 – 11

The tragic events of that day, 11 September 2001, caused by the destruction of the World Trade Twin Towers in New York, in which thousands lost their lives saw once more the re-emergence of the "Spirit of Arthur".

Rick Rescorla, a Cornishman from Hayle, was employed by the firm of "Morgan Stanley". He was responsible for security of the firm's 3700 employees in the World Trade Centre, 2700 of them employed in Tower 2.

After the second tower was hit Rick did, by the use of his strong calming voice and his singing of Cornish songs, manage to maintain order in the chaos and to save some 2700 people from certain death by leading them to safety.

Rick had collapsed from heat exhaustion at least once executing this mammoth task and was told during his strenuous efforts "Rick you have got to get out". He replied "I will as soon as I have got everybody else out". After getting all his people out he then returned into Tower 2 to ensure that none had been missed.

Rick was last seen 10 minutes before Tower 2 collapsed climbing upward from the 10th floor. **Cometh the hour, cometh the man.**

As neither the American or British governments had officially honoured this brave man, the Cornish Stannary Parliament therefore decided that the Cornish nation should honour its own.

A wax replica of an ancient Cornish cross was made by a member of the parliament and taken to the Wills family of The Blue Hills Tin Stream Works, St Agnes where a beautiful Cornish cross of pure St Agnes tin emerged from the moulding shop accompanied by a highly polished tin plaque to be later engraved.

When the Stannator mentioned payment the look of puzzlement and disdain upon the faces of both Mr Wills senior and Mr Wills junior made him realise that these men would rather have their hand cut off than receive payment for such work.

The pure Cornish tin cross was mounted upon a Delabole slate base and presented in a Cornish elm case to Susan Rescorla, Rick's widow, beside the memorial in Hayle erected in his memory where Mrs Rescorla said that she believed that her husband's bravery would in time be honoured "on both sides of the ocean" and that her husband received greater recognition in Cornwall than in the US. Rick was described by the Stannators present as symbolising the "spirit and soul of Cornwall".

THE FOREIGNERS OF CORNWALL

Cornwall means the *Cornu-foreigners* in old Anglo-Saxon English. 'Wall' is a contraction of *wallia,* hence also 'Wales' meaning foreigners. How Cornwall could simultaneously be described as 'foreign' and an 'English' county' can only be attributed to an early development of a distrust of foreigners; a charge often levelled at the Cornish themselves by the 'Englawallia'.

Cornwall described as a 'county' should also be seen against the background of the fact that between 1340 and 1800, the Kings of England claimed incorrectly, to be Kings of France. This passion for claiming other people's property has already been alluded to with regard to the Celtic King Arthur.

Only the French revolution and the execution of Louis XVI in 1793 seems to have induced a revision of the King of England's official titles.

During the Napoleonic wars, possibly by way of consolation for the apparent diminution of the King's status, the name of the *Mare Britannicum,* (British Sea) changed to the English Channel. At this time and presumably to halt the spread of disagreeable revolutionary ideas, the exemption of 'Stannary Regiments' from military service abroad was ended in 1802. (Militia Stannaries Act 1802 Chapter 72)

THE DUCHY OF CORNWALL

In 1337 A.D. the wealth of Cornwall as represented in its independent tin industry, was well known in Europe. There was no Duke in Britain before this European rank was introduced to establish the title, Duke of Cornwall. This Norman French Duke presumed to take over a Cornish speaking Celtic nation that was universally believed to have given birth to King Arthur.

It has been difficult for the academic world in England to make a thorough assessment of royal motives back down through the ages. The authors must agree with Anthony Barnett who wrote in *The Independent* of 20th August 1996: "Until the monarchy can be properly debated it will be hard to describe ourselves as a democracy".

The use of the title Duke imported from France and applied for the first time to tin rich Cornwall, was so important to the Norman French that it was made the prerogative of the first male heir and his heir of all future **Plantagenet** Kings for ever.

Acknowledgement of Cornwall's status is expressed in the Duchy Charter in the words; "remarkable places distinguished by their pristine honours". In association with the Stannary Charter of 1305, this Duchy Charter of 1337 represented an accommodation between England and Cornwall. The Stannary Charter of 1305 confirms the right "to do justice as heretofore in the Stannaries has been accustomed" and that the stannars "have all liberty, free customs and covenants above written without let or impeachment of Us, our Heirs, Justices, Sheriffs or Ministers".

Although nominally under Duchy of Cornwall jurisdiction, the Stannary organisation remained intact. Cornwall over a period of six centuries purchased its independence at the cost of billions of pounds sterling in taxes on tin, mineral rights and pre-emption rights claimed by the Dukes of Cornwall.

Pre-emption was a royal claim to the right to compulsory purchase of all production. The terms were negotiated with the Cornish Stannary Parliament. The extent of this transfer of wealth from a Cornish speaking people to a foreign monarchy was only mitigated by the influence of the Cornish Stannary Parliament and its Court of Stannary and Mines, the validity of which still survives to this day. There is ample evidence that the whole Duchy of Cornwall system was of doubtful legality both as regards Stannary Law and Magna Carta. The American researcher, G.R. Lewis, in his book *The Stannaries* (p. 83/4 - Harvard University 1908) affirms that the Norman Barons (1215) forced King John to renounce his claim to the Stannaries.

Why is the Duke of Cornwall not a Cornishman when the Duke of Luxembourg is a native of Luxembourg? It should also be noted that Luxembourg has retained its national identity at the centre of Europe during the wars of the twentieth century. This was not achieved by force of arms since there is only a population about the same as Cornwall. Its own official language is Letzeburgesch. Independence for Luxembourg was maintained because the majority of the nations of Europe were sufficiently civilised to extend the principle of respect to small nations and adopt the policy of live and let live which is unfortunately missing in relations between Cornwall and England.

The taxes on tin continued until 1828 by which time the Dukes of Cornwall had laid claim to extensive mineral rights, the income from which more than compensated for the lost tax on tin which was known as 'coinage'.

Although claiming 'the government of Cornwall' (Cornwall Foreshore Case 1858), the Duchy has not used the Cornish Court of Stannary and Mines to register claims to mineral rights, consequently Duchy of Cornwall mineral rights should now be regarded as 'Cornish public rights' if Magna Carta applies in Cornwall or Stannary rights under Cornish law.

Down through the ages the Parliament at Westminster and the monarchs themselves have preferred not to impose taxes on English people for the royal upkeep. This led to the search for the ideal method of obtaining unofficial income. Constitutional experts agree: "The principle that the King should live of his own had a double application; the sovereign who could dispense with taxation could dispense likewise with advice and co-operation". This is an astonishing quotation from *The Constitutional History of England* published by Clarendon Press, Oxford 1906. Did this financial 'principle' that the King should live by his own means, encourage monarchs with the tacit approval of Westminster, to ignore Magna Carta in Cornwall and to bend the rules to 'secure' a royal income from tin by accepting the jurisdiction of the Cornish Stannary Parliament? Is the wealth so amassed now called a 'private' estate"?

The historian, G.R. Elton in his *England under the Tudors* 1967, commented on the financial affairs of Kings. "The famous theory that the King should 'live of his own' found favour both with a people reluctant (to pay) and with a King desirous of making himself independent." Elton continues: "Most of the expenditure of the crown was no longer in any sense personal to the King; it was for purposes of state, and the nation in whose interests the money was spent ought to have contributed more formally to its supply". The Tudors did not wish to surrender freedom of action in exchange for (Westminster) votes for money."

As an indication of the wealth of the Stannaries, in 1495 an Italian Ambassador in London reported back to Rome. The diplomatic message went as follows: "The riches of England are greater than those of any other country in Europe. This owes in the first place to the great fertility of the soil. Next, the sale of their valuable tin brings in a large sum of money to the Kingdom". From *The Reign of Henry VIII* Volume II, by A.F. Pollard, University of London 1914. This information was recorded just two years before the Cornish Rebellion of 1497 led by An Gof and ending in the battle of Blackheath just outside London.

As with the rise and fall of every imperial power in history, the suppression, annexation and exploitation of small nations has usually been a process reversed by subsequent events.

"The English have used their propensity to violence to subjugate the smaller nations of Britain. Then we used it in Europe and with our Empire. So I think what you have in the UK is smaller nations who have been over the centuries under the cosh of the English" (Jack Straw - The Times Newspaper)

Did members of Parliament at Westminster turn a blind eye because an unofficial Stannary deal was preferable to returning to their constituencies and admitting to their electorate that they had agreed an increase in taxes to support the King and his family? Did the Cornish Stannary Parliament agree so that they could maintain their national identity? Has the bargain been kept? Has Cornish independence been respected? How could the result of a royal cross-border agreement now be called a 'royal private estate'? Is this far fetched description designed to avoid the question; 'Why have English people always been reluctant to pay taxes for their Royal Family?'

Such questions have never been asked in the English education system even though *The Observer* of 26th December 1993 published a public opinion poll which revealed that "73% want to axe the royals' state aid". No mention is made of Cornish aid to the Duke of Cornwall. Strangely no book has ever been written about the lives of the Dukes of Cornwall. Such a project could hardly present the long line of Cornish funded non-Cornish Dukes in a flattering light.

Should not The Duke of Cornwall be permitted to speak for himself? On a visit to Papua New Guinea in 1975, the Duke who is also Prince of Wales, heir apparent and Vice Defender of the Faith, stated his officially politically neutral views: "Everyone must obey the state authorities, for no authority exists without God's permission and the existing authorities have been put there by God. Whoever opposes the existing authority opposes what God has ordered and anyone who does so, will bring judgement upon himself". Does he therefore believe that the Cornish Stannary Parliament has been put there by God and that whoever opposes the existing authority opposes what God has ordered and anyone who does so will bring judgement upon himself?

On the other hand, over one hundred years ago in the Victorian Age and at the height of the British Empire, people were not afraid to question or scrutinise the role of the monarchy in society. Perhaps the elevation of royalty has become a substitute for the former business of administering an Empire.

Whatever the cause, the Victorians investigated the role of royalty with a great deal more intellectual honesty than is the case today. In 1850 the Solicitor General, referring to the Duchy of Cornwall, stated that he "could not discern this peculiar title and its connection with crown immunity". (*Royal Fortune* by Philip Hall 1992) Today such an assertion by the Solicitor General might well cost him his job.

In the House of Commons on 18 March 1872, Sir Charles Dilke said in a speech: "There is not likely to be made today any attempt to contend that the Duchy of Cornwall is the private property of the Prince of Wales". (*My Queen and I* by W. Hamilton MP 1975) Not many MP's would expect to

CORNISH STANNARY PARLIAMENT

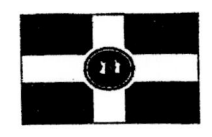

9 Coombe Park, Bal Lake, Camborne, Kernow/Cornwall TR14 OJG. Tel. 01209 710938

15 May 2000

INVOICE

The Earl Peel
The Lord Warden of the Stannaries
The Duchy of Cornwall
10 **Buckingham** Gate
London, SW 1E 6LA

To RECOVERY OF UNAUTHORISED OVERCHARGE ON TIN PRODUCTION IN CORNWALL BY THE DUCHY OF CORNWALL **contrary** to the **provisions** of **Magna** Carta, the **Stannary** Charters of 1305 & 1508, Duchy Charters of 1337/8, the Case of Mines 1568 & the Royal Mines Act 1693 AD **and without parliamentary authority.**

Period of Taxation by the Duchy of Cornwall.	Coinage/taxed	Size of units taxed	Total Cornish tin production in lbs.
1337 -1496 AD	21412	of 1200 lbs each	25694400
1504 - 1599 AD	61763	of 1200 lbs each	74115600
1600 - 1646 AD	23448	of 1200 lbs each	28137600
1647 - 1699 AD	**84090**	of 1000 lbs each	84090000
1700 - 1749 AD	167775	of 1000 lbs **each**	167775000
1750 -1799 AD	**267680**	of 1200 lbs each	321216000
1800 -1837 AD	246336	of 1200 lbs each	295603800
Total units taxed	**872504**	**Total production**	**996631600**

Cornwall - 872,504 taxable units of tin **production charged** @ £2.00 each.
England (County of Devon) - all units of tin **production** charged @ £0.78 each.
Difference due - 872,504 @ **overcharge rate of £1.22 per unit.**

Production figures taken from "The Stannaries by G.R.Lewis, Harvard University, U.S.A (1908).
Formula for **historic values** from **"The Sunday** Times**"** Rich List 2000. Coinage as % average historical GDP* by century x £865 billion (GDP 1999).

Century	Coinage Units	Overcharge (Units X £1.22)	Average historical GDP.	Overcharge as % of historical GDP	Overcharge in todays' values (1999)
1337 + 15th	21412	£26,123	£3.52 million	0.00742	**£6,418,300,000**
16th	61763	£75,350	£10.17	0.00741	**£6,409,600,000**
17th	107538	**£131,196**	£37.32	0.00351	£3,036,100,000
18th	435455	£531,255	£133.21	0.00398	£3,442,700,000
19th - 1837	246336	£300,530	£340.93	**0.00088**	£761,200,000

872,504 units overcharged @ £1.22 each + % GDP = £20,067,900,000.00

Final Total subject to agreement on V.A.T.   £20,067,900,000.00

E.&O.E. Terms:- 120 days.

survive such freedom of expression in today's climate where the English public does not want to know the truth about the monarchy and how they obtained their Cornish wealth.

The description 'peculiar title' with regard to the Duchy of Cornwall, was made without further explanation in "The Law Officer's Opinion of 18th August 1913" and to the House of Commons Select Committee on the Civil List 1972 (W. Hamilton MP – *My Queen and I*)

Philip Hall's final comment in Royal Fortune 1992 page 234 reveals the need to examine documents still classified as secret in order to extract the truth behind the facade of the Duchy of Cornwall. Philip Hall concludes: "It is even dubious whether the Duchy of Cornwall is owned by the Prince of Wales". There is every reason to believe that for reasons of suppressing the Cornish national identity, ample evidence lies hidden which would support the contention that the Duchy of Cornwall is the property of the Cornish people and should be held in trust by their own Stannary Parliament as the original owners. "Whilst subjected to repression enforced amnesia and identity realignment, their nation's legal personality was ferreted away, slipped into the Duke's back pocket to later emerge as a vehicle for profit" – Angarrack.

MINERAL RIGHTS

Of the many subjects where questions are discouraged in schools is the question of the history of royal financial activities. Great efforts are made to dismiss the question as prying into private affairs. Private? Why does the Limitation Act 1980 declare that "Nothing in this Act shall affect the prerogative right of Her Majesty or the Duke of Cornwall to any gold or silver mine"? Similarly, the Cornwall Submarine Mines Act of 1858 applies to the foreshore. Why are these assets claimed by the Duke of Cornwall in Cornwall and by the Crown elsewhere in the United Kingdom? This division of statutory state assistance between the Duke of Cornwall and the Crown also applies to *Bona Vacantia,* property of intestate, treasure trove and of course, mineral rights.

"His status as Duke of Cornwall transforms him into a fully functioning head of state. In fact it is of such significance and carries such authority, that it has to be separately empowered by over 150 Acts of parliament, each of which places him on an equal footing with the Queen in her jurisdiction. However, as the extant jurisdiction of the Duchy of Cornwall is recognised under the 1337/8 Charter as representing a British/Cornish survival of sovereignty, the head of state of the Duchy of Cornwall still represents the Cornish people and holds the land of the Cornish people in trust." (Angarrack)

So far as royal sovereignty is concerned, it will scarcely be contended but that the Duke of Cornwall was placed precisely in the position of King (Duchy of Cornwall 1855)

Is there an Act of the Westminster Parliament to support every other private estate by name? An article in the *Harpers and Queen* magazine of June 1994 by Jonathan Mantle, refers to constitutional theorists who argue that: "Crown Lands have been illegal since 1760". The author of the *Harpers and Queen* quotes a Duchy official as observing that Acts of the London Parliament enabled the Duchy "to do almost anything". There is silence as to where the Duke of Cornwall might "do almost anything" but then, where else but Cornwall? Some might consider a magazine report as a flight of fancy suitable to relieve the pain experienced in a dentist's waiting room. But no magazine will, it seems, ever reveal the whole story.

In the Cornwall Foreshore Case of 1858 involving a dispute between the Crown and the Duchy of Cornwall over the ownership of foreshore in Cornwall, the Attorney General to the Crown observed as follows: "Then it is said by the Duchy, 'we make the minerals ours by the act of extending the county by mining'. That one man should be able to change his neighbour's property into his own by committing a trespass upon the former is hardly consistent with the English or any other law". **Later in the case it is revealed that 'any other law' means Stannary law.**

EQUALITY BEFORE THE LAW

Throughout the Cornwall Foreshore Case of 1858, the Attorney General to the Crown insisted that the Duke of Cornwall could not expect to be treated any differently than any other of Her Majesty's subjects.

Of particular relevance to the acclaimed principle of equality before the law which applies to American Presidents and their wives, would be the obligation to register a Duke's claims to mineral rights in the same manner as that stipulated for 'tinners at large' to register their 'bounds' or claims.

The concept of equality before the law is completely missing from the Cornwall Foreshore Case of 1858 as no Stannary representatives were called to give evidence at this special "Trial at Bar" reserved for royal disputes.

While institutionally avoiding the concept of equality before the law which should equally apply to the Cornish, the credentials of democratic leadership by England appear to be missing an equal and fair legal foundation as they clearly do not provide the constitutional right to cultural equality to all.

This is a serious matter since Prince Charles, Duke of Cornwall has spoken these words: "Whoever opposes the existing authority opposes what God has ordered and anyone who does do, will bring judgement upon himself". The Duke of Cornwall does not inform his listeners that the ultimate authority in this world is the International Court of the United Nations at The Hague, Holland or the European Court of Human Rights at Strasbourg, France.

Questions must at least be raised and answered when official legal documents refer to the Duchy of Cornwall as "a mode of descent unknown to the common law". (*Halsbury's Laws, Volume & Constitutional Law* paragraph 1560 published 1993)

THE CASE OF MINES

In the Case of Mines of 1568 the judges decreed that the income from the Stannaries was intended for administration purposes and not for the profit of the Dukes. This was legal recognition of the fact that **since the Tudors had ended the Plantagenet dynasty by killing off Richard III, non-Plantagenets were not entitled to the fortunes accruing from the original Plantagenet Duchy of Cornwall Charter.**

The Plantagenet Duchy of Cornwall Charter claimed the Stannaries of Cornwall. Yet, if the Stannaries had been already renounced as royal property by King John in compliance with the ruling of the Norman Barons according to G.R. Lewis above, was this claim also made outside the provisions of Magna Carta? *Halsbury's Volume 8 Constitutional Law*, paragraph 1058 states: "By Magna Carta the Crown is restrained from making grants in derogation of public rights". While the prescriptive rights of the Stannaries are well established, it is particularly revealing that the Tudor King Henry VII never claimed ownership of the Stannaries.

The Case of Mines 1568 was ignored in the Cornwall Foreshore Case of 1858. Neither the 'caretaker' ruling of 1568 nor the Baron's rejection of 1215 was permitted to detract from a royal claim of 'inheritance', unknown to the common law in 1858. The Duchy submission in the Cornwall Foreshore Case 1858 asserts: "The Lordship (ownership) of the county (Cornwall) which Edward I had inherited from Earl Edmund comprised the Stannaries of the county and inferentially from that the general ownership of the soil throughout the county".

County is a word derived from comunitatis, meaning community which when applied to Cornwall, signifies the Cornish Nation as depicted on the Stannary seal on the front cover of this book.
To describe Cornwall as if it were a county of England would be to deny its true constitutional status of being the land of the original indigenous people of Britain, a land and people separate from England.

In the late 1800's there was a failure to legally incorporate Cornwall into the shire county system of England.

In the Foreshore Case 1855, the UK government conceded that the word comunitatis (county) is sometimes used to signify a **territorial possession** as distinguished from the division of the kingdom for civil purposes as stated in the case of the Duchy.

OWNERSHIP OF THE SOIL

If the Stannaries are actually the basis for the claims of the Dukes of Cornwall to the "general ownership of the soil throughout the 'county'", then but for that royal claim, the general ownership of the soil of Cornwall would lie indisputably with the Stannaries. No wonder the Lord Chief Justice, Lord Tenterden put on record in 1831: "The estate of the Duchy of Cornwall is one of a very peculiar nature; there is nothing like it existing in this country". (Rowe –v- Brenton, Concanen Edition 1831)

The Cornwall Foreshore Case 1858 involving a dispute between the Monarchy and the Duchy of Cornwall over the Foreshore of Cornwall, reveals legal opinion that: "as the Stannary unquestionably extended over the whole 'county', it is manifest that the term Duchy was used in an equally extensive sense". Neither this passage nor its quotation by Doctor Philip Payton in *The Making of Modern Cornwall* page 67, make any comment on the fact that since the Stannaries existed centuries before the Duchy was created, then any claims by the Duchy in Cornwall have to be reconciled with prescriptive rights under Stannary law.

Doctor Payton omits 'as' at the beginning of the quote which causes confusion in deciding which claim takes precedence in prescriptive right and Magna Carta.

The Cornwall Foreshore Case 1858 produces other surprises
The Attorney General to the Crown submitted: Before tracing further the history of the Earldom (before the Duchy in 1337) it is proper to draw attention to one species of property in this 'county' almost peculiar to it and essentially connected with its soil, namely the Stannaries or tin mines there and from a few particulars of their history, some light will be thrown on the main question in this case, namely to whom the ownership of soil of the 'county' belonged in early times". He continues: "There is no express

reference to the tin mines of Cornwall in *Doomsday Book*". *Doomsday Book* is of course the book in which all Crown property was recorded and an entry is used as proof of such ownership. The *Doomsday Book* was compiled in 1086.

So how could the Duchy claim the Stannaries? What bias causes the English education system to fight shy of the Duchy of Cornwall and the Stannaries? What use was Magna Carta if it could not protect the freehold land of the subject against rapacious royal personages?

The Cornish, having previously made an accommodation with the Norman French whereby in exchange for a percentage of the profits from their tin metal, would continue their own form of governance which had existed since time immemorial. The Cornish were therefore not subjects of the English crown.

TERRA NULLUS – UNCLAIMED LAND

Colonial pioneers have often claimed land as *terra nullus*. The Duchy of Cornwall has apparently, for example, used this legal definition to claim the Isles of Scilly. However, this royal claim is disputed on a number of grounds.

The Duchy itself in the Cornwall Foreshore Case 1858, admitted that the "Isles of Scilly" had been "omitted" from its Charters along with a number of other important items subsequently claimed by the Duchy. The Attorney General to the Crown asserted in 1858, that the law required that anything not entered in the Duchy Charters of 1337 could not be claimed as Duchy property.
We note that there are a number of examples where the American government has paid compensation for land taken from the natives of the soil of America. This practical economic recognition of the right of small nations to survive is not considered either a necessity or a virtue in Britain, despite pious claims of a multi-cultural society.

The current Westminster Duchy of Cornwall Management Act 1863 to 1982 section 37, declares the "rights" of the Duke of Cornwall in Cornwall.

"Possessions shall include, regalities (royal privilege) lands, commons, mines, minerals, stone, substrata, castles, rights etc. etc. whether in possession or reputed or claimed to be parcel of the Duchy of Cornwall. "This would seem to indicate that the Duke of Cornwall is entitled to claim just about anything he fancies in Cornwall at any time.

These existing feudal laws lie behind the scenes while the public relations spin doctors present the Duchy as a fine example of private enterprise. But where is the history of the land before the Dukes of Cornwall and what is the basis of their claim? In fact the Duchy of Cornwall is a government department (*Whitacker's Almanac*) which is busy denying its own existence.

Without indulging in poetic licence the reader might find it interesting to decide whether the sentiments expressed in this very old proverb of Celtic wisdom are applicable to the Duchy of Cornwall:

> "*The law doth punish man or woman*
> *Who steals the goose from off the common?*
> *But lets the greater thief run loose*
> *Who steals the common from the goose.*"?

If the Duke of Cornwall's feudal claims are backed by Westminster, then is Westminster supporting exploitation to the racial advantage of the English majority in Britain?

In keeping with best international practice of recompense for small nations, there appears to be a case for these properties to be returned into the administration of the Cornish Stannaries by and for the Cornish people. Notwithstanding Cornish prescriptive rights, such a 're-claim' of land and mineral rights should be based on implementation of the Magna Carta provision: "no freeman may be deprived of his freehold, liberties or free customs." *Halsbury's Constitutional Law* Volume 8 para 909)

Westminster sovereignty does not appear to defend the rights of Magna Carta in Cornwall.

The Westminster Duchy of Cornwall Act 1844 section 84 states: "Nothing in this act shall extend to any lawful right, profit or privilege to which the tinners (Stannary Community) of Cornwall are or claim to be, entitled by force of any statute, custom, prescription or royal charter".

GOVERNMENT WITHOUT CONSENT

The Duke of Cornwall has since 1337 been described as a title belonging automatically to the heir to the throne regardless of the fact that in 1485 in the Celtic conquest of England, Richard III, the last Plantagenet, was killed by Henry Tudor thereby ending any legitimate future claims to the Dukedom (Duchy) of Cornwall.

In the Cornwall Foreshore Case 1858, the Attorney General to the Duchy of Cornwall affirmed: "The Duchy Charters vested in the Dukes of Cornwall, not only the government of Cornwall but the entire territorial dominion previously vested in the Crown".

It is appropriate to compare the foregoing statement with that in *Halsbury's Constitutional* Laws 1993 volume 8 paragraph 902, which states: "the exercise of the prerogative by the rightful heir out of possession is void and of no legal effect" – paragraph 902 of constitutional law. This indicates that the Duke of Cornwall in his capacity as heir to the throne and therefore out of possession, cannot exercise the royal writ in the United Kingdom without having the writ declared void and of no legal effect. If this were correct, then it would be illegal for the Dukes of Cornwall as heirs to the throne, to issue writs in Cornwall as they did to create 44 Westminster constituencies (Duchy rotten boroughs) or to claim the Isles of Scilly. However as Dukes were entitled to exercise the prerogative and issue writs in Cornwall, then Cornwall was not being governed as part of the United Kingdom but rather directly or indirectly as a land extra-territorial to England by the Dukes of Cornwall.

Within a Cornish context, the only control ever exercised over the Dukes of Cornwall and accepted by them, has been through the Cornish Stannary Parliament.

CONVENE A PARLIAMENT AT YOUR DESCRETION

The position of the Cornish Stannary Parliament, convened as it is at present, without a writ of the Duke Cornwall, is nevertheless on a firm foundation. As revealed in *Carew's Survey of Cornwall* 1602, Edmund, Earl of Cornwall 1272 to 1300, authorised the Stannators by Charter, "to manage all Stannary causes and for that intent to hold Parliaments at their discretion".

The date of this Stannary Charter is obscure but since the Stannary Seal is not mentioned until 1225, it is fairly safe to conclude as affirmed by Sir George Harrison, Keeper of the Records of the Duchy of Cornwall in 1835, that "Stannary Charters" from English sources "only confirmed pre-existing rights and privileges even then of ancient date" – "Your fellows shall be your judges and arbitrators (Constantine C700AD).

If the writs of the Dukes of Cornwall in Cornwall were in fact illegal in English law, then Magna Carta did not apply in Cornwall. However, if the Dukes represented a government of colonial caretakers, then they would be subject to the authority of the people of that territory which in terms of historical precedent and ownership of the soil, is represented by the Cornish Stannary Parliament. The area of the Stannaries has always been the same as the geographical area of Cornwall.

The British Museum Stannary Manuscripts reveal that the Dukes always accepted the statutes of the Cornish Stannary Parliaments chiefly in order to secure their income. Even the income from land and property was administered by the Court of Stannary and Mines up to 1896 when the venue and function of this court was transferred to the Cornwall (County) Court.

THE ABOLITION OF COURT PROFITS FOR THE DUCHY

Stannary advice was not solicited for the Stannary Court (Abolition) Act 1896. This act did not and could not abolish Stannary Law. It was designed to abolish the fines, confiscations and profits of the Court of Stannary and Mines paid to the Dukes of Cornwall. **To this day the Dukes**

still receive annual compensation for this and other losses of income from the Stannaries. The Duke had also established himself as the court of final appeal in Stannary cases, a role that royal image-makers wanted swept under the carpet through the abolition of the Dukes' feudal functions within the Stannaries. Claims to Stannary profits by the Duke of Cornwall had been specifically rejected in the Case of Mines 1568. (*Plowden's Commentaries* 1761)

THE CELTIC CONQUEST OF ENGLAND

Students are encouraged to remember William the Conqueror 1066 but in 1485 "Henry the Conqueror" is studiously discouraged.

Only the eminent historian A.F. Pollard, has put Henry VII under the heading "Invasion and conquest of England". *(The Reign of Henry VII from contemporary sources* 1485-1509 volumes I, II and III by A.F. Pollard M.A. Professor of English History, London University 1914)

Pollard's work provides great insight into the Tudor period. He observes: "The Speaker alone of the Commons may speak in the Parliament chamber; His regular petition for freedom of speech is for himself alone". This means that Members of the House of Commons did not have the right to freedom of speech. Pollard also noted: "The power of making positive law could only develop in royal hands".

With regard to Henry VII's legal title to the crown, Professor Pollard declares: "Distant as Henry Tudor (Henry VII) was from the direct line of successors to the English crown and dubious as his retention of it long appeared to be, the throne afforded him the only prospect of tolerable security". Pollard further quotes reports made by the Spanish envoy: "He keeps the people in such subjection as has never been the case before". That was in 1498 just one year after the Cornish Rebellion of 1497 which proclaimed Perkin Warbeck, King Richard IV at Bodmin. Obviously like the education system today, embarrassing events in Cornwall would not be discussed in the best of circles in London lest they offend the King and incur retribution on his behalf.

Unfortunately the one-eyed view of history as justification for contemporary political thinking, prevented even Professor Pollard from recognising that what had happened five hundred years ago was the **Celtic conquest** of England by a Breton, Cornish and Welsh army, leading to the unique right of the Cornish to **veto** English statutes.

Although some historians have claimed that the veto is applicable only to matters involving tin or perhaps the Stannaries, there is nothing in the Charter of Pardon 1508 to restrict the veto to any English legislation.

THE CORNISH RIGHT TO VETO ENGLISH STATUTES

The Charter of Pardon 1508 is one of the most significant in providing substance to the case of the Stannaries and its presentation for anyone looking into the untold history of Britain.

The Charter of Pardon 1508 provides for the Cornish Stannary Parliament, the right to veto any provision or statute issued by anyone claiming authority under the Crown or the Duke of Cornwall. The Charter actually states: "no act or statute etc. shall have effect in the Stannaries without the assent and consent of the twenty four qualified men of the Stannaries".

There is nothing in the Charter of 1508 to restrict the right of veto to any particular type of English law therefore, it applies to all English law relevant to Cornwall.

CHARTERS IN INTERNATIONAL LATIN

Most English Charters, including Magna Carta, were written in Latin. As with the Duchy Charter 1337, there are some serious mis-translations in rendering the Latin text into English. In the Duchy Charter, the English version of *Curia Stannaria et Minera* is given as 'Stannary Court' whereas, even a layman in this case, can see that 'Court of Stannary and Mines' is more accurate.

It is possible that the mis-translation was an attempt to assist the Duke with regard to the thousands of acres of mineral rights which he claims as personal property in Cornwall, but which have not been registered with the 'Court of Stannary and Mines'.

Apart from Stannary law, English law has set a precedent which should apply to all connected with tin. The Dukes themselves since they were 'connected' with tin, would be classified under the Charters as a 'tinner at large'. In the case of tin 'bounders' or people making a tin claim, the English courts have ruled in the case of Rogers –v- Brenton 1847 (Brenton being the Duke's agent contesting bounding rights) "that to register claims for tin without working the tin was unreasonable".

If the same Stannary bounding law was applied to Duchy claims to mineral rights, then mineral rights claimed by the Duchy, would be void as 'unregistered' and/or 'unreasonable' for not being worked.

It is strange that the Duchy, while claiming the 'government' of Cornwall did not recognise the Cornish Court of Stannary and Mines but selected the English Courts as the line of least resistance and racial solidarity, to gain possession of property in Cornwall without interrogation in an open Cornish Court of Stannary and Mines by Stannary witnesses.

Was the Court of Stannary and Mines transferred to the Cornwall (County) Court in 1896 in an attempt to assist the Dukes of Cornwall in their cover-up of very weak claims to land and mineral rights in Cornwall?

In the Stannary Charter 1508 casus has been translated as 'occasion' whereas the Stannaries translates it as 'emergency'. Since the Charter mentions the death of Arthur, the King's first born son on four occasions (even though he had been dead for five years) and does not

Charter Day

mention the second son, Henry (the future Henry VIII) as being the new Duke of Cornwall, the silence of English academics on these points must be the subject of investigation.

The omission of the word 'emergency' from the English translation leaves the impression that a final selection of nominated Stannators remains permanently in the hands of the Mayors of the four Stannary towns, Launceston, Lostwithiel, Truro and Helston which were in fact centres where newly smelted tin had to be taken quarterly by producers to pay Duchy taxes and were known as 'Coinage Towns'. Helston for example still has a Coinage Hall Street and Truro its Coinage Hall.

The text literally provides for an *ad hoc* meeting of the twenty four 'legitimate and qualified' men of the Stannaries to give their 'assent and consent' to Westminster statutes as they arise and consequently, the role of 'Duchy appointed mayors' was not permanent but a 'cooling off' temporary solution to meet the Tudor emergency.

Selection of nominees by the mayors and aldermen of towns was also the prescribed method of choosing members of Parliament at Westminster at that time. In Cornwall the administration of this procedure was under the Dukes of Cornwall. Such a system would have no validity when compared with the prescriptive rights of 'deciding among yourselves' or modern constitutional law.

THE CONSTITUTION OF CORNWALL

On 7th September 1993, the Cornish Stannary Parliament published its booklet *The Constitution of Cornwall or Kernow, the Country of the West Britons*. It is a statement of the reasons for a continuing Stannary Parliament with quotes from relevant Westminster Acts and an introduction to the legal arguments. There is also a comparison of identical phrases used in the 1337 Duchy and 1508 Stannary Charters.

Copies were sent to media, academic and cultural institutions along with representative public bodies in Cornwall, Britain, Europe and America.

RACE RELATIONS

The Cornish Stannary Parliament is one of the founder members of the 'Commission for Racial Equality in Cornwall'. The objective of members at the Commission's meetings in Cornwall is to obtain the application in Cornwall of the provisions of the 'Framework Convention for the Protection of National Minorities'. At the inaugural meeting on 4th July 1996, the then Chairman and Speaker of the Cornish Stannary Parliament, Ray Pascoe is reported in the *West Briton* 11th July 1996 as saying: "We feel that the Commission should take into account all colours of racism in Cornwall, not merely black; there is blatant discrimination against Cornish people".

If people do not affirm their own nationality, then others will assume that they belong to another?

United Nation Declaration on the Rights of Indigenous Peoples - Sept. 2007

Article 1 - Indigenous people have the right to the full enjoyment, as a collective or as individuals, of all human rights and fundamental freedoms as recognised in the Charter of the United Nations, the Universal Declaration of human Rights and human rights law.

Article 3 - Indigenous people have the right to self-determination.
Article 4 - Rights relating to matters of internal and local affairs.
Article 5 - Right to strengthen their own political, legal, economic, social & cultural institutions.

Article 8 - (1) Indigenous peoples and individuals have the right not to be subjected to forced assimilation or destruction of their culture. (2) States shall provide effective mechanisms for prevention of, and redress for:-
(a) Any action which has the aim or effect of depriving them of their integrity as distinct peoples, or of their cultural values or ethnic identities; (b) Any action which has the aim or effect of dispossessing them of their land, territories or resources; (c) Any form of forced population transfer which has aim or effect of violating or undermining any of their rights; (d) Any form of

education authorities are fighting a rear-guard action to prevent English people from suffering the shock of discovering the truth about their own roots.

In his three volume historical survey *The Reign of Henry VII*, Professor A.F. Pollard observes: "The English constitution is not easy to define at the present day; (1913) it was still more difficult in 1485 and no satisfactory attempt has been made to determine what was and what was not constitutional during the 'Tudor period' ".

Despite being party to the writing of a constitution for Iraq, the British 'unwritten constitution' may be more accurately described as a 'nonstitution'

The moral integrity of such falsehoods does not seem to equate with such wondrous humanitarian and benevolent deeds as the England dominated Westminster government portrays to the wider world.

Why is it that Cornish history and its constitutional position is being ignored, suppressed, misrepresented or given superficial treatment? How can a modern people not know their constitutional position?

'Scales of Justice' – *The Times* 6th July 2011 states: "For 796 years since Magna Carta, judges in this country have played a vital role in upholding the unwritten constitution. They guarantee protection to each individual against arbitrary action by the state. The current ranks of the judiciary include some of the best minds of a generation. At the very top of the profession, people such as Lord Judge and Baroness Hale of Richmond, combine integrity, intellect and independence with an emotional intelligence that gives them insights into the anguished, flawed or furious human beings who come before them. Yet the caricature of the remote pompous judge is not without substance". The Times also states: "A British judge has been elected to the top judge at the European Court of Human Rights in Strasbourg. The choice of a Briton is unlikely to calm increasing political concerns in Britain".

The trend in Europe is to increase the power of the regions and Cornwall loses out if it is prevented from taking its rightful place as one of the Celtic regions of Britain and Europe.

The magazine of the *European newspaper* 15-21 August 1996 carried a full feature on the United Kingdom. In an article entitled *State of the Nations*, Ray Connelly contributes: "So what are we, English or British? Or to an Englishman, are both concepts one and the same thing? It's a terrible arrogance but I suspect so. *The Scots, Welsh and Irish, even the Cornish, I suppose have a narrower sense of cultural identity arising out of the ghosts of their vanquished pasts*".

The European movement towards cultural diversity and regional self-government is recognition that past victories are not forever and that large states can no longer deploy gunboat diplomacy or argue a case for racial supremacy.

Presentation of a case is usually through the media whose exercise of editorial control means less and less 'live' and therefore 'open' debates. In a recent case the Cornish Stannary Parliament sought to obtain a signature from a BBC reporter that he agreed to comply with the Royal Charter of the BBC. This was refused but later reported as: "The Cornish Stannary Parliament were invited to contribute to this programme but imposed conditions the BBC felt were unreasonable".

The Royal Charter or Constitution of the BBC is described in a BBC publication as follows: "Whereas newspapers are at liberty to editorialise on any subject they choose, the broadcasting authorities are specifically prevented from doing so. The notion of impartiality is at the very heart of the BBC". (The BBC Charter Article 13)

There is apparently no attempt to reconcile the disparity between this promotion material with the day to day running of the service. The concept of leadership by example is not apparent in the action of certain public institutions.

Despite the age of 'Information Technology' and the worldwide availability of information on the international 'Internet', the BBC and the English

The Constitution of Cornwall or Kernow was the subject of a request for legal deposit copies from the libraries of the Universities of Oxford and Cambridge, the National Library of Scotland, the Library of Trinity College, Dublin and the National Library of Wales in May 1994.

This present publication is designed to add to and expand upon the information contained in 'The Yellow Book', the popular name for the Constitution.

Under the Cornish Constitution, the rights of all the citizens of Cornwall are protected by the European Convention of Human Rights and United Nations Declaration of Human Rights. Subsequent protocols and associated international treaties such as the 'Framework Convention for the Protection of National Minorities', will be included by constitutional amendment.

Since the international court at The Hague, Holland is accepted as the ultimate court of appeal by the British government, then the United Nations' 'Declaration of Human Rights' which The Hague Court upholds, must be considered as the ultimate law by the British government and Westminster Parliament.

The Westminster Parliament has incorporated the Human Rights Convention into domestic law but has produced its own version entitled 'The Human Rights Act' which supposedly 'mirrors' the European Convention on Human Rights, but with the blatant omission of Article 13 and other alterations. Article 13 in the European Convention on Human Rights provides for a remedy against official discrimination, however in the England Human Rights Act Article 13, like their constitution, is unwritten. The supremacy of European law ensures official discrimination is countered in their written Article 13. Does the acclaimed sovereignty of the Parliament at Westminster mean that it can ignore Magna Carta and international treaties on human rights among which the 1508 Charter of Pardon may be considered to be such?

Since Magna Carta and Human Rights are, for practical purposes not recognised in domestic law, while in addition there is no written constitution or constitutional court, what is there to prevent official racial discrimination against the Cornish?

assimilation or integration; (e) Any form of propaganda designed to promote or incite racial or ethnic discrimination directed against them.

Article 9 - (1) Indigenous people and individuals have the right to belong to an indigenous community or nation in accordance with the traditions and customs of community or nation concerned - with no discrimination.

Article 11 - Indigenous people have the right to maintain, protect and develop past, present and future manifestations of their cultures, such as archaeological and historic sites, artefacts, designs, ceremonies, technologies and visual and preforming arts and literature. (2) States shall provide redress through effective mechanisms re violation of their laws, intellectual property, traditions and customs.

Article 13 - The right to transmit to future generations their histories, languages, oral traditions, and to retain their own names for communities, places and persons.
Article 14 - Indigenous people shall have the right to establish and control their education systems and institutions providing education in their own languages.
Article 16 - (1) Indigenous people shall have the right to establish their own media. (2) State owned media shall duly reflect indigenous cultural diversity.
Article 18 - Right to participate in decision-making in matters affecting their rights.
Article 26 - The right to the land, territories and resources they have traditionally owned.
Article 27 - States to establish independent and impartial procedures.
Article 28 - Restitution for land etc taken without their free, prior and informed consent.

UK government in support stated: "The UK did not accept that some groups in society should benefit from human rights that were not available to others. With the exception of the right to self-determination, the UK did not accept the concept of collective human rights in international law." "National minority groups and other ethnic groups within the territory of the UK and its overseas territories did not fall within the scope of the indigenous peoples to which the Declaration applied".

Wapedia - "The term indigenous people or autochthonous peoples" (1) "can be used to describe any ethnic group of people who inhabit a geographic region with which they have the earliest known historical connection". (2) "Association with a given region before its subsequent colonisation or annexation".

Summary by Cornish Parliament, March 2009

THE CAMELOT IMAGE

Was Henry VII's first-born son called Arthur after the legendary Celtic King Arthur as a public relations stunt to enhance the prestige of the new Tudor dynasty?

Was it consequently a shock or in medieval terms, the curse of the gods that this son in whom so much expectation had been placed, failed to create an Arthurian Tudor age? Was the death of Prince Arthur in 1503 the real emergency that left the Tudor King Henry VII without a claim to the Duchy of Cornwall resources of tin and Camelot?

The exclusion of Henry, the second son of Henry VII from the Charter of Pardon 1508 to the Stannaries of Cornwall and the listing of 'doubtful' (*journal of the Royal Institution of Cornwall* 1915) for the date on which this second son, later Henry VIII, became Duke of Cornwall after the death of his brother Arthur in 1503, indicates a Tudor emergency at this time. Did the later academic reference to 'doubtful' indicate that legally the Tudor title to Duchy of Cornwall assets expired with the Tudor elimination of the Plantagenets? Legal and historical references are carefully deferential about Royal entitlement and Duchy entitlement to Cornwall and the Stannaries but should not the question be put: Is there not a Cornish entitlement to Cornwall and the Stannaries?

The focus of investigation is the modern legal definition of the Duchy of Cornwall as: "a form of descent unknown to the common law", Henry VII must have been aware of this problem confronting him as the usurper of the throne, a situation which would undermine the legality of future Dukes of

> Prayer Book
> Rebellion
>
> HEMM A GOVHA AN KOLL A
> GOLLJI GLASNEDH HA'N
> MERNANS A VILYOW A
> WLASKARORYON GERNEWEK YN UNN
> DHEFENDYA A GA FYDH, YETH
> HA DEVOSOW KELTEK
>
> THIS COMMEMORATES
> THE LOSS OF GLASNEY COLLEGE
> AND THE DEATH OF
> THOUSANDS OF CORNISH PATRIOTS
> IN DEFENCE OF THEIR FAITH, LANGUAGE
> AND CELTIC CUSTOMS.
>
> 1549 – 1999
> KERNOW ARTA

Glasney Stone

Cornwall. Is this why he concluded an agreement with the Cornish Stannary Community after failing to secure their compliance by other means?

As the Cornish had provided a large contribution in his army of conquest (of England) was Henry obliged to provide a fair proportion of the spoils of war by way of a continuing recognition of Cornish independence?

Henry VII at least recognised a Cornish entitlement to Cornwall

The death of the Tudor Arthur had lasting implications, whether by divine providence or not. An already insecure Tudor dynasty in the superstitious Middle Ages must have been devastated by the apparent adverse judgement of God. This bad omen was an emergency of the first order.

On his succession to the throne, Henry VIII married Catherine of Aragon, the former wife of his elder deceased brother Arthur. Perhaps this was an attempt to revive the Camelot image with the new King walking in Arthur's footsteps. Catherine's subsequent failure to produce a son and Tudor heir after twenty three years led to further speculation on divine providence in a witch hunting age.

The survival of the Tudor dynasty hung in the balance. The solution of divorce was made possible by the creation of the Church of England as the government department for religion.

The Church of England was established by the simple expedient of the King authorising the confiscation of all other churches and religious property. King Henry VIII could now break with tradition and sanction his own divorce.

The fiction of English chivalry was exposed as being thoroughly divorced from the original Celtic Arthurian quest for the Holy Grail.

Eventually Henry VIII married five more wives under the rules of his own new church for which he decided he was 'Defender of the Faith'. Unlike the real live Henry VIII, no King in the age of chivalry as in English fiction or Hollywood films had actually executed two wives. The Tudor attempt to dress up in Arthurian legend had made a farce of chivalry by using royal divorce, charges of treason, a nationalised Church acquired without compensation and the execution of people for dissent in the quest for hereditary perfection.

There is no record of the defence put by the executed and divorced wives of Henry VIII. The King was assumed to be above the law on the side of God. This was the divine right of Kings. The King could do no wrong.

Even today criticism of events and decisions in royal history is often attacked more fiercely than criticism of religious history. Fiction has replaced fact. In the Tudor rape of Camelot, wives had become a disposable commodity. Henry VIII married Katherine Howard on the day, 28th July 1540, that he had his Prime Minister Thomas Cromwell, executed. These events along with the 72,000 executions during Henry VIII's reign must have had a lasting psychological impact on the English population and reinforced the unwritten constitutional feature of complete and absolute obedience to a monarch's wishes as God's representative on earth.

Not until the present day has the Church of England again sanctioned a royal divorce, this time for Charles Philip 'Arthur' George, Prince of Wales and Duke of Cornwall. Edward VIII married a divorcee and had to abdicate.

The present Duke's names could hardly have been chosen at random. Philip is the name of his father and George his grandfather. Charles signifies the association of his grandmother with the Scottish Stuart dynasty so where did 'Arthur' come from? A win with the existing national lottery, run by a company called 'Camelot' would not be necessary to finance investigations into the royal reason behind the selection of 'Arthur' for Prince Charles.

ANGO-SAXON CULTURE

In his book *The Anglo-Saxon Age*, Longman 1973, D.J.V. Fisher reveals what he describes as the character of conquest. "Many of the characteristics of Roman Britain had disappeared during the long period which elapsed after the departure of the Roman army and before the German conquests." The Germanic conquests featured the Anglo-Saxons who later

Trevithick Engine

became known as the English from Angle-ish. Around 500 A.D. this conquest was successfully resisted by a Celtic hero known as King Arthur.

"From Anglo-Saxon times, the English had sought to dominate the whole of Great Britain, and this desire for domination increased from the mid-13th century." This statement is a quotation from the book *Britain's Heritage* by J.J. Norwich, Granada Publications 1983, which stands out as a confession not encountered in English history books for schools.

All too often there is an unseemly assumption of racial superiority coupled with the arrogance inherent in the campaign by some English people to dress themselves up in the mantle of the Celtic King Arthur. Even the 'National' lottery is run by yet another latter day Anglo-Saxon 'Camelot'.

Hollywood too has fallen into the racial trap with descriptions like: "Arthur was the greatest of all English Kings". Is this a case of any un-researched nonsense to provide false glories and false pride for the Anglo-Saxons that Arthur sought to defeat?

By falsely assuming ownership of Cornish history and depriving the Cornish and the Celts of their heroes, the Anglo-Saxons are making it easier for those of their number who claim that the Cornish have nothing and are too ignorant to achieve anything. This type of racial abuse amounts to accusing the victim of a robbery of having nothing.

The abuse has moved into the area of providing some commentators with a superficial superiority complex. Speaking on CBS news of America in July 1996, Simon Bates, formerly of the B.B.C., is reported by Media E of San Francisco as saying: "The Cornish are ignorant inbreds". Simon Bates is obviously unaware that the Cornish are the oldest industrial nation of Britain and have through their great intellect in the field of invention, literature and the arts, given the world its first railway locomotive, first blood transfusion, such discoveries as nitrous oxide (laughing gas), the doubling of the known elements, the discovery of the planet Neptune and a hundred other firsts. Perhaps people such as Simon Bates should continue to entertain children and keep away from grown-up subjects.

Although the American *Readers Digest of Modern Knowledge* rightly accredits the invention of the steam locomotive to the Cornishman Richard Trevithick 1803, the politically controlled English history curriculum teaches that it was the Englishman George Stephenson 1825. Stephenson was depicted on a five-pound note. One concession has been to depict Trevithick on a limited number of two pound coins.

There is also the state funded English Heritage, English Nature and English Partnerships active in Cornwall with a mandate to assimilate Celtic Cornwall into Anglo-Saxon England. English Partnerships have now been re-branded as the 'Homes and Communities Agency' who have acquired large amounts of land in Cornwall for mass house building. This will even further increase the proportion of English people to Cornish people within Cornwall – 58 sites in Cornwall, 2 in Devon and 1 in Somerset.

The England dominated Westminster parliament appears to be blatantly and purposefully disregarding European and International Treaties with impunity in order to assimilate the Cornish people into an England that does not exist on the western side of the Tamar.

Cornwall Council has reduced the number of new homes stipulated by Westminster and the new figure proposed is 68,000 plus but only a small portion of this is required for local needs. This plan is in direct conflict with the Framework Convention for the Protection of National Minorities signed by the British government in February 1995. Article 16 states: "The Parties (governments) shall refrain from measures which alter the proportions of the population in areas inhabited by persons belonging to national minorities". Research by COSERG, a Cornish scientific research group, estimates that only 1600 homes are actually needed for local Cornish people.

NO VICTORY LASTS FOREVER

Those who travel around the world will notice that there is much to be learned about the art of self-analysis.

The England brand of bias lies in the denial of their roots and the assumption that claimed victories last forever. Therefore they say, the Celtic nations of Britain can never be trusted with self-government within a federal system. The English interpretation of democracy they say cannot be improved. Meanwhile indigenous racial minorities throughout Europe have the freedom to develop in their own style.

This refusal to break with past-alleged victories has created a bias which prevents acceptance of cultural diversity. The English expect a one-culture society, a concept which runs contrary to the tide of history. It is imperialistic and out of touch with reality.

This problem for the Celts of Britain can be described as the one culture mentality or the English bias virus. It is as destructive of the mental software of the victim as that of any computer virus. The unfortunate victim indulges in psycho time travel. For example, if 1900 is considered to be the most glorious year of the imperial age to which the victim is attached, then this age is projected forwards or backwards in time to create a sense of well being. The facts are not important. Those going back in time can imagine an England before England existed, as during the Arthurian age or when singing Blake's *Jerusalem* without answering the question – 'and did those feet in ancient time walk upon England's mountains green? The answer of course is that at the time of Christ, there was no England as there was only Britain and the Britons. Those projecting forward in time need not concern themselves as to why Orders of the British Empire are being awarded when the days of the Empire are past.

Sky TV Monday 3rd October 2011 – Time Team documentary Malton; "The intrepid archaeological team head for a picturesque village in North Yorkshire where a bed of nettles conceals 2000 years of English history". Even historians cannot it seems resist any chance to back date Englands history to a time when England did not exist.

At the present time there is stubborn silence from the BBC and government departments about introducing the Framework Convention for the Protection of National Minorities signed by the British government on 1st February 1995. The Convention establishes that people of small nations have the right "to seek funds for the establishment of media, as this right is considered self-evident".

As yet acceptance into the Framework Convention of the Cornish has been denied by the England dominated Westminster parliament. The English bias/virus blinds their officials to the fact that the Celtic Cornish are a nation in their own right (from pre-England times) and having resided on their own territory for millennia, can in no way be described as English or residing in England "A division of races older and more original than that of Babel, keeps this close esoteric family apart from neighbouring Englishmen." – Robert Louis Stevenson

The people rated by Bodner as being most like the ancient Britons are those from Cornwall. By contrast Bodner assumes the people most likely to be Anglo-Saxon in origin are those from East Anglia and Lincolnshire, the first places to have borne the brunt of those waves of incoming Saxons. From the latest genetic study of the peoples of Britain entitled 'Face of Britain.

What kind of education system encourages English people to believe that they are either Britons or indigenous?

There is also a distinct reluctance to accept that Cornish place names and surnames are Celtic and not English.

The British public are not kept up to date with international developments in extending Human Rights to combat the abuse of power by politicians and other leaders of a state. Progress in this field includes the United Nations International Covenant on Economic, Social and Cultural Rights and the International Covenant on Civil and Political Rights which British politicians have accepted at international conventions but apparently delete them from policy plans on arrival back in the UK. There are also many treaties by the nations of the Council of Europe to protect the rights of small nations.

Putting the state's official signature to treaties, according to a written reply from the Foreign and Commonwealth Office, Human Rights Policy Department on 15th April 1996 means: **"States are obliged to give effect to the obligations they have assumed under any treaty to whch they are a party in accordance with the provisions of international law"**. The imperialist age may have been racist to the degree of ignoring international commitments but that fortunately is no longer legally possible.

It is abundantly obvious that not all English men or women suffer from racial bias. There are some English people who are Cornuphile and do all they can to beat back the arrogance of imperial spin doctors in London who have nothing better to do than mess about in every detail of Cornish affairs.

Lord Robin Teverson, the then Member of the European Parliament for Cornwall and Plymouth, in a letter dated 16th September 1994 stated: "I do not regard Cornwall as part of England. Cornwall has a separate cultural and historic identity and should always be treated in such a way".

AN ENGLISH PORTRAIT OF ENGLISH RACISM

At least one English sociologist has made observations about the content of the English history curriculum in schools. Ann Dummett in her book *A Portrait of English Racism* published by Pelican Books 1973 – ISBN 0 14 12 1607 3, remarks: "It is almost impossible for English people to accept or understand the truth about their country's past". She also observes: "English people have been by and large, educated in a fitting manner for an imperialist destiny". At the present time "with very few overseas territories, the one obvious place for the imperialist destiny to find its expression, is within England itself". In her introduction, the authoress states that her use of "English" rather than "British" is for reasons of accuracy.

Cornwall not being within England continues to be treated as if it were an overseas territory but is in fact a British territory far older than the territory known as England.

Under these circumstances, Cornish people would be particularly foolish to fall victim to English misinformation about their Cornish history and their unique Cornish Stannary heritage. The Stannaries are a tradition of the Celtic world which does not fit in with the state controlled English education system in Cornwall because it is the key to Cornish national self-esteem and the right to self-determination in an improved democratic system.

THE BRITISH

Britain is comprised of four nations, three Celtic and one Anglo-Saxon. They are the Cornish, Scots, Welsh and English. The English the only non-Celts, have a numerical majority. This Anglo-Saxon racial majority has created a 'unitary' as opposed to federal state. Britain has no written constitution and there is still an un-elected, undemocratic House of Lords promoting an English nationalist version of British history.

These very unusual constitutional features tend to ensure English dominance in every political and cultural activity in Britain. In America it would be as if the large state of New York were permitted to use its numerical majority to impose its will on the smaller states of Connecticut, Maine and Delaware. Additionally if by way of comparison, the people of those states were of a different race, then naturally there would be a 'self-evident' case for negotiations to establish the rights of all races and cultures. In an American context such negotiations would revolve around the equal representation afforded to both large and small states in the US Senate.

English historians are in the habit of referring to Cornwall's Celtic identity in the past tense. The Cornish are the original Britons and have been resident in Britain long before the English invaded Britain. Cornish place names and surnames still exist to this day. Cornwall is entitled to a **Celtic future.**

At the present time the school curriculum for history is decided by English politicians and is made compulsory in Cornish schools. The daily use of Cornish Celtic place names and surnames continues regardless and without the benefit of comparative cash investment, compared with the millions of pounds spent on educating English people to use their own language correctly. The Cornish Language Partnership has been set up and is funded by Cornwall Council and Communities and Local Government. This funding has enabled the Partnership to teach the Cornish language and set up classes in many areas of Cornwall for those wishing to learn the language. The teaching of the English language in Cornish schools is compulsory – the teaching of Cornish is not – WHY?

In general the British can accept accents whether an, Australian, Indian, Scots or Welsh but the local BBC television is at pains to avoid including a Cornish accent for local news programmes. It all sounds like an English Broadcasting Corporation.

Could English people be so embarrassed by the loss of the British Empire that they now seek to build an English Empire in Britain?

THE TEUTONIC KNIGHTS

English Heritage is a state subsidised organisation for the preservation of ancient and modern monuments. It receives £120 million per annum from the government. Cornish Heritage is not recognised and gets no official funds. English Heritage operates its assimilation policy in Cornwall by attaching English Heritage signs to Cornish Celtic monuments. Even pre-English Stonehenge is claimed as English. Eager to prove his

English rather than British nationality, the Duke of Cornwall has leased Tintagel to English Heritage. This act of national dressing up in the Celtic clothes of King Arthur and Camelot follows the Tudor example of trying to boost an usurper's image at any price.

English dictionaries attempt to promote an English cultural supremacy by describing Camelot (in Arthurian Legend), "an English town where King Arthur's palace and court were situated" (*Collins Concise English Dictionary*). Since Arthur or a Celtic war lord in about 500 AD, devoted his life to the defeat of the Anglo-Saxon English invaders of Celtic Britain, this is a direct racial insult to the Celts of Britain revealing the true colours of the dictionary as Collins English Nationalist Dictionary.

The *Sunday Times* of 26th May 1996 carries a front page report announcing that Prince Charles, Duke of Cornwall, spoke of his wish to be seen as 'Defender of Faith', rather than 'Defender of the Faith'. However, the Prime Minister is reported as warning Charles of "an empty gesture" by suggesting a role for himself as 'Defender of Faith'.

Incredibly there is only English Heritage, there is no state funded British Heritage organisation. This deliberate omission exposes indifference bordering on an insult to the sacrifices made in two world wars by members of the 'British' Armed Forces.

Why is it that the English education system does not teach that the Anglo-Saxon English are part of the Teutonic English/German race? What about St. George and the Dragon? The patron saint of England was a Turk and lived long before the word England came into use. Whatever happened to the English/German Order of Teutonic Knights of Henry II 1154 – 1189? These were the Crusaders defending Christianity. *The Story of England* by A. Bryant, Collins 1961

Why discard a genuine English 'Order of Teutonic Knights' in favour of adopting the Celtic Chivalry of King Arthur as if he were English?

THE WHOLE DUCHY OF CORNWALL DECLARED FORFEIT

The period 1485-1509 should be described as 'The Celtic Conquest of England by Tudor Henry VII' and sub-titled as a national emergency. There was also the refusal of the Cornish to accept Tudor Duchy of Cornwall statutes and regulations, their refusal to pay the King's taxes for war against Scotland and their armed march on London. All this was compounded in 1503 with the death of Arthur the new Tudor King's firstborn son. The name 'Arthur' had been specifically chosen to enhance the status of the new Tudor dynasty by association with the legendary Celtic King Arthur and his Camelot Court.

The statutes of Arthur Tudor, pretender Duke of Cornwall, in 1496 as rejected by the Stannaries, are listed in the *Journal of the Royal Institution of Cornwall* Part 1 1915 page 71. Under these circumstances it is difficult to believe that the Cornish were prepared to accept the Mayors of the Duchy controlled coinage towns, as Stannary representatives for the duration of the emergency. Although disputed in some quarters, this is confirmed in the Charter of Pardon 1508. Duchy control of elections in the coinage towns is confirmed in an article by Graham Haslam in the *Journal of the Royal Institution of Cornwall* 1980 page 226.

It is also of some significance in relation to the question of who had the right to inherit the Duchy of Cornwall and its assets after the elimination of the Plantagenets, that the Tudor King Henry VII "declared forfeit the whole Duchy of Cornwall". This means, surrendered to or taken as a penalty by the King. It does not mean taken into personal royal ownership since the Tudors unlike the Plantagenets, never referred to the Stannaries as 'our Stannaries'.

The terminology used in the Stannary Charter of Pardon of 1508, appears to confirm the cancellation or forfeiture of Duchy Charters. The text consolidated for clarity reads: "For the enjoyment of these our said grants; any acts, statutes or proclamations made by whatsoever authority before these times shall be revoked, annulled and annihilated in accordance with the advice of the aforesaid Cornish Stannary Community, and their heirs and successors, for their best profit and advantage". Therefore Henry VII had annihilated the three charters of Creation of the Duchy of 1337/8 due to his annihilation of Richard III, the last Plantagenet in his conquest of England in 1485 and had therefore rendered those charters redundant.

It would appear that all subsequent Dukes have held their Dukedoms by "right of might" rather than by chartered right.

The 'forfeiture' or confiscation is revealed in the *Stannary Manuscript* at the British Museum number 6317 page 136. The evidence suggests that this situation was resolved with the conclusion of an agreement "between the King and the whole Stannary Community", namely the 1508 Charter of Pardon giving the Cornish the right to veto English statutes, proclamations, acts and provisions.

Significantly, there is nothing in the 1508 Stannary Charter of Pardon to suggest that the Dukes of Cornwall were entitled to collect a tax of coinage on tin or claim mineral rights. Since the taxes on tin were nevertheless collected by the Duchy under the jurisdiction of the Cornish Stannary Parliament, the unavoidable conclusion is that all Duchy claims to property and mineral rights in Cornwall are only legal if sanctioned by the Cornish Stannary Parliament.

No evidence is available to suggest that any Duchy claims have been sanctioned by the Cornish Stannary Parliament. It would seem that any Duchy claims have been illegal for over 500 years promoting a foreign hierarchical autocracy in place of legitimate democracy.

CONFIDENCE IN THE MONARCHY

If there is an English myth, it is that royalty can do no wrong, at least if they ever did do it, then it should be hidden from view. The forfeiture by the King of the whole Duchy of Cornwall has been hidden from view. The passage in the *Journal of the Royal Institution of Cornwall* 1915 by J. Blake M.A., under the title The Cornish Rebellion of 1497, fails to quote the British Museum text in full. All the interesting pieces are quoted except "the forfeiture of the whole Duchy of Cornwall".

This same event is described euphemistically by Dr. Philip Payton as "Henry VII's suspension of the Stannaries" in his book *The Making of Modern Cornwall* page 59. In fact this same book often quotes the Cornwall Foreshore Case 1858 only as Duchy documents and without revealing that the case concerns a dispute between the Crown and the Duchy of Cornwall over the Foreshore of Cornwall. Omitted from all academic revelations is the Crown's rejection of Duchy claims as "adverse to the title both of the Duke and of the Crown". Certainly English scholars are too intimidated by the educational establishment to investigate the proposition that the Duchy of Cornwall did not comply with the provisions of Magna Carta.

Why is it that even after nearly five centuries, the 'Celtic emergency' of the Tudor usurpation of the Crown of England and the subsequent calamitous death of the first son and heir to the Tudor dynasty, namesake of the legendary Arthur, there is no investigation into the weakness of Duchy claims to property in Cornwall? Does this 'Conquest of England' upset the game plan of presenting English history as a 'divinely inspired succession of monarchs'? In other words history from an English perspective is designed to protect the reputation of ancient and modern royal personages and exclude the British dimension.

If the British public were confident in the political neutrality of the monarchy, they would probably be found a role as 'Defender of the Constitution' in place of the assumed feudal title 'Defender of the Faith'. The royals in the role of 'Defenders of the Constitution' would be obliged to prepare and introduce the best constitution in the world along the lines of the European and United Nations Convention of Human Rights with their guarantees of freedom of expression for all ideas, even on television.

A modern constitution like that of Sweden, recognises that one numerically superior race within a given democratic system could not publicly justify discrimination against other smaller races within the same system. Consequently to avoid the abuse of numerically superior power in a civilised society, Article 15 of the Swedish Constitution states: "No act of law or other statutory instrument may entail the discrimination of any citizen because he belongs to a minority on grounds of race, skin colour or ethnic origin".

Such official discrimination by politicians as lawmakers is not unconstitutional in Britain. (Due to Britain's unwritten constitution).

THE BALANCE OF POWER

After the first World War 1914-1918 and the introduction of the Order of the British Empire, external dangers and xenophobic propaganda prevented a radical assessment of the functions of government, even retrospectively back down through history.

Little significance has been given to the fact that Henry Tewdar (Welsh spelling) later to become the Tudor, Henry VII, not only invaded England but actually did so from a Celtic country with a Breton, Cornish and Welsh army. Henry Tudor had spent fourteen years in exile in Brittany where he obviously had time on his hands to learn Breton. Coincidentally Breton happens to be a language derived from the Cornish who had migrated to Brittany to escape the English attempted conquest of Britain that commenced in c.450 A.D. and continuing at various levels up to the present day.

1560 years of continuous attempted subjugation of another people must be considered a "violation of human rights"

Commenting on the validity of Henry VII's claim to the throne of England, A.R. Myers of Liverpool University in an article published by The Historical Association June 1968, concluded: "The title of Henry VII was so weak and there were so many conspiracies against him, that he needed all the justification for his accession that he could find". This included naming his first-born son 'Arthur'>

Legal justification and legitimacy of birth were also weak in the extreme when it came to the desire of the Tudors to inherit the wealth of Cornwall claimed by the previous Duchy of Cornwall.

Although the Cornish did not always see eye to eye with Henry's policies, it is not inconceivable that following the death of his first born son Arthur, he was anxious to make an agreement which had a chance of remaining intact for future generations of Tudor Kings. How could the Tudors remain independent of the Westminster Parliament by avoiding the need to summon a session to raise taxes when there was no legitimacy for a Duke or Duchy? The Stannary Charter of Pardon was concluded in 1508 just one year before Henry VII died.

In the end, did Henry realising that the Duchy Charter of 1337 legally applied only to the Plantagenets, declare "the whole Duchy of Cornwall forfeit" and make a new start by coming to an arrangement with the Cornish which he did not honour?

If this was a new start, then the Charter of Pardon of 1508 to the Cornish Stannary Community begins to take on the significance of a treaty. It would also mean that royal continuity since Henry VII is dependent upon the 1508 Stannary Charter. The fact is that a grant of a Charter of Pardon is the prerogative of a monarch and cannot be repealed by the Westminster Parliament any more than Westminster can convene itself. However, if the right to veto English law by the Cornish was an attempt to break the stranglehold of centralised power, then it was premature. Henry VIII effectively banned the Cornish language by declaring that all loyal subjects should speak the English tongue, (28 Henry VIII c.10 1536). In the cause of religious freedom the Cornish revolted in 1549 as they had done in 1497 against the King's taxes for war against Scotland and the bogus Duke of Cornwall's statutes to tax the Stannaries. There then followed the incursion into Cornwall of Henry's death squads. It has been estimated that up to 1/5 of the Cornish population was subsequently put to death (sanctioned by the Church of England).

The opportunity for the movement of power away from the centre has only recently been given new impetus with the European Framework Convention for the Protection of National Minorities and the Charter for Local Self-Government. At present the only movement discernible in the UK is the moving outwards of a 'Government Office for the South West' to reinforce central control over every detail of Cornish affairs.

The Times newspaper is the acclaimed mouthpiece of a self-interested political class. On 6th August 1996, it reported in an article on language; "It's not because Cornishmen are inscrutable that they look at you in that way. It's just that they can't understand half of what you're saying". For the hard of understanding, the author of the above appears to be culturally challenged. If the Cornishman appears unmoved when the said author speaks, it is because the Cornishman's culture dictates that if he does move, it may be fast and painful for said author!

If the above article had substituted 'African' in place of 'Cornishmen', it would at least have elicited a politically correct and unbiased response condemning racial abuse. In a democratic country, the people are citizens not subjects.

Did not the eminent English philosopher John Stuart Mill observe: "There is only one thing worse than a tyrant and that is a band of tyrants"?

CONVENED BY WRIT OF THE DUKE OF CORNWALL

Although there is nothing in the Stannary Charter of 1508 to allow such action, the Cornish Stannary Parliament was until 1752, convened by writ or order of the Duke of Cornwall. Royal power was absolute, dictatorial would not be inappropriate. The infamous Star Chamber or Royal Court acted only on what the King perceived to be the law. *The Haydn's Dictionary of Dates* 1868 reveals that there were 72,000 executions during the reign of Henry VIII. An article published by the Historical Association in February 1968 quotes from *The English Reformation* by Professor A.G. Dickens reveals "Nationalism within the English Church grew in strength throughout the medieval centuries". Was the Church being used as a tool of the state to sanctify the stature of an unpopular dynasty?

All Duchy prerogatives, writs or orders were certainly in conflict with Magna Carta. Royal authority was absolute until 1760 when Crown estates were surrendered to the British nation in exchange for a permanent salary from British tax payers through the consolidated fund. The property of the Duchy of Cornwall was not at the same time surrendered back to the Cornish nation, as should have been the case.

Until 1832, Cornwall was represented in the House of Commons part of Westminster, by forty four Members of Parliament, one less than for the whole of Scotland which had about six times the population of Cornwall.

How could this happen in a land claiming to be the oldest democracy in the world?

The abuse of power exercised by the Duchy of Cornwall hardly knew any bounds when it came to creating new wards or constituencies for the House of Commons part of the Westminster Parliament.

The overwhelming majority of those elected were from outside Cornwall, many were current or former Duchy officials. Even with the Reform Act of 1832 Cornwall returned (or was it the Duke of Cornwall who still returned?) , about twenty members to the House of Commons at Westminster. At present there are six. Before 1900 Westminster Parliamentary representation for Cornwall in the House of Commons could accurately be described as dependent upon Duchy Rotten Boroughs.

The phrase 'Duchy Rotten Boroughs' is not in use to describe the manipulation of election results. It would be more appropriate on this side of the Atlantic than borrowing the commonly used Americanism, gerrymander. Perhaps ignoring certain facts about one's own history helps promote the belief that dirty tricks only happen abroad.

The Reform Act of 1832 apart from the unreformed and unelected House of Lords, was in some way to bring Britain into line with the more advanced principles of Greek democracy operating in America.

The Dukes of Cornwall discontinued issuing writs or orders to convene a Cornish Stannary Parliament in 1752. The Stannary Parliament of 1750 had asserted it rights to the full and it is assumed that such conduct was sufficient to withhold the Duke's writ. International conflict and fear of royal censure prevented progress until the cause was taken up by Brian Hambley in 1974. Regrettably Brian Hambley died in 1985 but not before he had established the validity of Stannary law in a memorable series of court cases.

WHY A STANNARY PARLIAMENT NOW?

In 1974 Brian Hambley realised that whereas the Parliament at Westminster had relinquished its right to convene at its discretion, (16 Charles II chapter 1 1664) with great foresight, the Cornish Stannary Parliament had not followed the Westminster example. The Cornish Stannary Parliament was again convened in 1974.

It was further discovered that Cornwall was still entitled to its Parliament by prescriptive right and even in English law, *Hailsbury's* Volume 12 para 444): **"A custom is not destroyed by mere lapse of time during which no act of enjoyment has occurred".** A Cornish Stannary Community has been established as the electoral college for nominations and elections.

Of particular interest is the fact that in 1977 the Lord High Chancellor of Great Britain, the highest legal authority, confirmed the current validity of the Stannary Charter of Pardon 1508.
The Cornish Stannary Parliament represents a denial of the traditional version of British history. It is quite clear that the paths of the Stannaries and the Duchy have for so long been locked into an international contest to determine whether the Cornish or the English should run Cornwall. Is it not strange that English people want to believe that no such contest ever existed, while the Cornish struggle against an hypocrisy which widely proclaims its defence of the right of small nations, that is, wherever and whenever, as long as they are not within the Islands of Britain?

It should be noted that English commentaries employ the word 'tinners' in an attempt to play down the significance of the Stannaries. All Charters are in Latin and it is therefore inappropriate for modern English people to dismiss the Latin word 'Stannaries' by translating it as merely 'tinners'. The Stannaries were an alternative meaning for Cornwall as an organisation administering the overwhelming part of the national wealth and covering mines and tinners. Why did the English desert their own language to write Charters in Latin if it were not to ensure accuracy? If 'tinners' were accurate why is 'tinners' not in the original?

Most English people are not taught that approximately one quarter of the English language comprises words borrowed from Latin. There is no attempt to translate these borrowed Latin words into a less than accurate English word. What would be the English for A.D. *Anno Domini* - in the year of our Lord or *post mortum* – after death or *omnibus* – for everyone. So why 'tinners' instead of Stannars or Stannators or Stannaries?

In his book *Cornwall in the Age of the Industrial Revolution*, Dr. John Rowe, University of Liverpool 1953, makes this observation about the Stannaries: "It is possible that the earliest Plantagenet Charters to the tinners (Stannary Community) were not grants of privileges and immunities so much as limitations of older and wider jurisdictions; jurisdictions which had embraced every type of (legal) case, criminal as well as civil and may have been based on Celtic rather than on English 'customary' law".

With regard to Charters about Cornwall, legal representatives of the Crown in the Cornwall Foreshore Case 1858 declared: "It is probable, moreover, that these charters were only a recognition of a previously existing custom or right, in the inhabitants of Cornwall, as it is obvious that neither the King or the Earl (later the Duke), nor both could have legally made such a grant de novo (as of new) as to the lands of other barons, knights, and landowners in the 'county'". Evidently legal opinion for the Attorney General had Magna Carta in mind when he drew such a conclusion against independent action by royal personages.

Professor Pennington in his introduction to *The Laws of the Stannaries* reprinted 1974 from the original of 1760, describes the Cornish Stannary Parliament as "A legislature with powers parallel to those of the Parliament of Westminster". Professor Pennington continues: "The power to veto legislation by central government if it affected tin mining". Tin mining is the English translation of "Stannaries" Celtic/Latin. There is no evidence in the Charter of Pardon 1508 (where the right to veto English legislation is granted) which supports the Professor's conclusion that the veto was restricted to matters of tin only.

Nevertheless, Professor Pennington concedes: "No other institution has ever had such wide powers in the history of this country". This would indicate that the pre English Stannary Legistation would have been the model adopted by the later English Parliament, (afterall the Cornish were described as being civlised in c310 B.C.).

There is a significant difference in perception between English and American academics. Adding a new dimension to the politics of envy, English people who had never heard about the wealth of Cornish tin, not surprisingly, dismiss the tin business as an historical sideshow. In reality the solution may lie with those Cornish men and women who can find the time to cross check the source of the information on which they base their conclusions.

For the American, as in the case of G.R. Lewis of Harvard University in his book *The Stannaries* 1908, objectivity is the order of the day. Lewis observes: "That the Stannaries, here meaning of course the mines themselves rather than the political organisation which rose about them, must date to a remote period in antiquity at least to the Bronze age, is practically undisputed".

The American two-fold definition of Stannaries as a political or governmental body as well as the administrator of mining activities is supported by reference to documentation in respect of at least one Stannary area as the local government. In contrast, that the Duchy authorities failed to translate correctly from their Charter the name of the Court of Stannary and Mines, is evidence of the Duchy role in attempting to remove all traces of Cornish independence from the record.

The official list of reference documents for 'Mining' provided by the Duchy of Cornwall reveals some interesting omissions. The Cornwall Foreshore case 1858 is excluded. This reveals assertions by the Duchy that it was the 'government' of Cornwall, held land belonging to the Stannaries and admitted the omission of the Isles of Scilly from its Charters which according to the testimony of the Crown, negated Duchy claims to ownership. Also excluded from the list is The Case of Mines 1568 revealing the Duchy in a **caretaker** role or **servant** of the Cornish public rather than a personal profit making organisation for the Dukes of Cornwall.

MINING TODAY

Cornwall's last working mine, South Crofty, was unfortunately closed in 1998. The increase in the price of tin has made it a viable proposition again and work has been continuing for some time to re-open the mine and it should be back in full production very soon, Blue Hills tin stream near St. Agnes is still producing tin to this day which means that tin production in Cornwall has never ceased over the past 4000 years.

In the meantime, it should be noted that the authors of the Charter of Pardon 1508 were not only anxious to preserve the right of the heirs and successors of future Kings but also in the manner of a treaty, the reciprocal rights of the heirs and successors of the members of the Cornish Stannary Community who struck a bargain with King Henry VII. This embraced the right of the heirs and successors of the Cornish Stannary Community of 1508 to convene the customary Cornish Stannary Parliament at their discretion.

HEIRS AND SUCCESSORS

The heirs and successors of the Cornish Stannary Community are just as much in the picture today as are the successors of the Tudor dynasty. The twenty-four Stannators meet regularly to discuss affairs and, if applicable, ratify the actions of the Constitutional Committee who deal with urgent matters when they arise. The Stannary Charter of Pardon of 1508 clearly gives to all heirs and successors of 'stannars' or 'seekers of tin' or 'tinners at large', the right to participate in the Cornish Stannary Community and elections to the Cornish Stannary Parliament.

FREEDOM OF SPEECH

Since April 1995 the Cornish Stannary Parliament has been trying to extract an answer from the BBC about its position with regard to the Framework Convention for the Protection of National Minorities, signed by the British government in February 1995.

Not only does this European Minorities Convention provide the right of access to television media by national minorities, it further considers under Article 9, that it is 'self evident' that a national minority should have the right to "establish media and to seek funds to do so". An answer from the BBC would require a statement acknowledging that under Article 8 of its Royal Charter, it is required to implement the provision of all international agreements relating to broadcasting.

It would appear at present that The Framework Convention for the Protection of National Minorities is being ignored by official bodies to achieve English racial advantage.

Naturally Stannary elections without the free access to the television media afforded to English political parties who all promote the assimilation of Cornwall into England and accept foreign donations to promote their campaigns, would mean that having wrestled free of the Duchy of Cornwall, the Cornish Stannary Parliament could possibly fall into the hands of one or other of the highly visible English political parties. The English media has often appeared over enthusiastic in promoting the **official party line that Cornwall is part of England as opposed to part of Britain.** There is also a tendency for the media to usurp the rights of the Cornish to choose their destiny. No approval has been given by the Cornish people to permit the inclusion of Cornwall into an English South West Region or a West Country Region. Cornwall is widely accepted as the Celtic country of the West of Britain. At least the *Western Morning News* conducted a public survey which revealed on 13th June 1996 that 70% of the sample of 700 Cornish people wanted some form of 'Home Rule' or independent self-government.

Unfortunately the English media is geared to prevent disclosure of the fact that Cornish people have a legal and inalienable chartered right to their own parliament including a right to veto any English law that is detrimental to Cornwall or Cornish people.

CORNISH UNIVERSITY CHALLENGE

Despite a long and difficult campaign to achieve a Cornish University Cornwall has been fobbed off by having imposed upon it an English University.

The University of Exeter has opened a University in Cornwall and has been challenged to show its intellectual credentials by the Cornish Stannary Parliament. Will it sweep Cornish history under the carpet? The challenge requires answers to some culturally sensitive and historically taboo questions focused around the proposition that "The English education system should stop manipulating Cornish history".

The fact that no answers to these questions have been received, exposes the possibility of autocratic tendencies in academic circles.

PETITION TO THE EUROPEAN PARLIAMENT

In March 1994 the European Parliament declared admissible, the petition submitted to them by the Cornish Stannary Parliament The petition comprised a detailed analysis of the case for the Celtic industry, heritage, traditions and economic welfare of the Cornish people. Despite sending copies to the media, no detailed report was published explaining the reasons for this appeal to our European Community who would act as an independent jury.

Again the media, dutiful to their masters in London, fulful their role in the attempted assimilation of Cornwall into England through the **denial of knowledge** to the Cornish people.

PART OF EUROPE'S HERITAGE

If Cornwall is not considered part of British Heritage by the English majority in Britain, at least the European Commissioner for Regional Policy, Frau Monika Wulf-Mathies provided a written statement of her position in May 1995. "I support the need to reinforce the languages and identities of minorities throughout the Community thereby strengthening the cultural richness and diversity that is part of Europe's heritage." The letter concludes: "We hope that the Stannary Parliament will be able to play its full role in this" (Regional policy).

Although the Cornish Stannary Parliament presented its case to secure membership of the South West European Grants Monitoring Committee, it was turned down by the Government Office for the South West who, following a later enquiry were prepared to state that it was not policy to "assimilate" Celtic Cornwall into Anglo-Saxon England. The Cornish Stannary Parliament will be seeking practical implementation of the government's stated non-assimilation policy.

In practice at the present time, the policy of assimilation appears to be intensifying rather than diminishing.

The Duchy of Cornwall has a seat on the South West European Grants Monitoring Committee and is also a recipient of European grants. No Cornish cultural organisation is represented.

"Tony Blair believed that the Prince of Wales publicly interfered in sensitive areas of government policies in a manner that sometimes stepped over the constitutional boundaries historically respected by the Royal family according to Alistair Campbell" – *The Guardian* 2nd July 2011.

The Single Programming Document of the European Union on grants policy for Cornwall expressed the conviction that "the unique and extensive remains of mining and engineering activity are being recognised as an historical industrial heritage of international importance".

CORNWALL NEVER LEGALLY INCORPORATED INTO ENGLAND

Throughout 1994 the Cornish Stannary Parliament submitted statements to the Local Government Commission for England which had announced its intention to re-organise local government in England and Cornwall.

The government's preferred plan was to abolish all District Councils and leave only the County Councils. This has been controversially imposed and Cornwall became a Unitary Authority in 2008. In 1995 after a meeting between the Commission and the Constitutional Committee of the Stannary Parliament the final report of the Commission contained this statement under the heading of *History and Culture*. "Some suggest that Cornwall has never legally been incorporated into shire England and the continued existence of the Stannary Parliament for Cornwall encourages this thought particularly within a Europe of Regions".

Although this statement is probably a manifestation of a bureaucratic compromise, it nevertheless by its inclusion, reveals a reluctant admission of the non-English constitutional position of Cornwall at a time when European influence is beginning to penetrate the outdated attitudes towards minority nations that pass for toleration in the United Kingdom.

As Cornwall was excluded from the union between England, Wales and Scotland in 1707 due to Cornwall being extra territorial to England, the Cornish nation therefore cannot be constitutionally described as British in the modern sense (since 1707) but remains a nation separated from the three nations included in the union.

"Cornwall has no chance in hell of securing a public enquiry into protecting its historic boundary with Devon. Proposed legislation has finally received Royal assent following marathon sessions in parliament. It will be impossible for the boundary commission to do anything about it even if it says that Cornwall should not be split up. In the final debates, Andrew George Lib Dem PM for St. Ives, criticised the inflexible and rigid re-drawing of the boundaries. He said the lack of a Cornish amendment was a result of the intransigence of the Prime Minister". Western Morning News 18th February 2011

It must be assumed that Royal assent has been granted by the Duke of Cornwall as the Queen of Britain is unable to give Royal Assent to any decision by her parliament regarding the territory west of the Tamar. The Duke must be well aware that constitutionally any such decision by the Westminster parliament must receive ratification by the Cornish Stannary Parliament in order to have legal effect.

THE TRIAL THAT NEVER WAS

Heritage – That which is handed down by ones ancestors.

After 1983 the archaeological sites in Cornwall formerly in the care of the 'Ministry of Public Buildings and Works' were inaccurately and misleadingly renamed English Heritage. This was with no consultation or consideration of the fact that any heritage to the west of the eastern bank of the Tamar is **Cornish Heritage**. Many of the archaeological sites predate both England and the English people by over 5000 years.

Bolowall Barrow the burial place of an important Cornish ancestor was constructed thousands of years before the existence of English people.

Chysauster Ancient Village was built, occupied and abandoned long before England or English people existed.

King Doniert's Stone commemorates a Cornish King who successfully fought against the Saxon English and so on.

The unconstitutionally newly formed English Heritage swept into action, signs were erected at Cornish Heritage and archaeological sites stating that these Cornish sites were now English Heritage. Revised guidebooks were distributed to tourist offices, libraries, schools etc. while the English school curriculum (force fed to Cornish children) studiously omits references to or instruction in the vast history of Cornwall's technological, artistic, musical, astronomical etc. contributions to world development, let alone a vast history of persecution, resistance and resilience leading to the continuing existence of the Cornish as a nation.

After repeated requests by the Cornish Stannary Parliament for English Heritage to remove their offensive signs from Cornish Heritage sites, a final ultimatum was delivered – "Remove your signs and return them to their country of origin or the Cornish Stannary Parliament will". The ultimatum was ignored.

The first offensive English Heritage sign was removed at Chysauster Ancient Village on 20th January 2000 by Stannary Bailiff, E.R. Nute with Assistant Bailiffs, H. Rowe and W.D. Nute and returned to its country of origin 'English Heritage Offices, Bristol, England' at 2.30pm on the same day.

The same sign reappeared affixed to Chysauster Ancient Village site some time later. English Heritage was then notified that if the signs were not removed then they would be confiscated. The English Heritage signs remained. Subsequently the sign at Chysauster plus 17 other English Heritage signs from other Cornish archaeological sites were removed and confiscated by the Cornish Stannary Bailiff and Assistant Bailiff H. Rowe. W.D. Nute later died after a short illness of a 'very rare form of a very rare disease'.

During this period the local press put out a statement that "English Heritage signs were being stolen and that a Police Officer had been allotted to each sign".

Upon reading this press statement, the Stannary Bailiff was very puzzled because English Heritage had been notified of the forthcoming confiscation by the Stannary Parliament and immediately following the removal of each English Heritage sign, a statement appeared upon the Cornish Stannary Parliament website detailing the confiscation, site, time of removal etc. by the Cornish Stannary Parliament. A letter detailing the same was also immediately sent to the English Heritage offices in Bristol, England, therefore there was no doubt as to who was confiscating the English Heritage signs or why.

A Cornish Stannary Parliament press release stated – *"the signs have been confiscated to be held as evidence of English cultural aggression in Cornwall. We understand from previous correspondence that you are as anxious as we are to act within the law, consequently you will no doubt be pleased that we have taken the time and trouble to have your inaccurate and misleading signs removed from public view".*

The Stannary Bailiff decided to visit Camborne Police Station. Upon arriving, he approached the duty officer at the desk and said, "Good Evening, I understand that you are looking for the persons that are removing English Heritage signs". The duty officer said, "Yes we are". "Well" said the Bailiff, "I am the person that is cutting down and confiscating those signs". The duty officer then said, "Excuse me" and walked back around the corner. The Bailiff could hear the murmur of voices. In a while the duty officer returned and instead of being arrested, the Bailiff was informed "thank you very much for your information, I will inform the appropriate officer". The Bailiff left Camborne Police Station even more puzzled than when he had entered it. The duty officer had not even asked for his name.

The Bailiff and Assistant Bailiff together with the Stannary's legal advisor and photographer in attendance, continued to confiscate English Heritage signs, duly notifying English Heritage on each occasion.

Arriving at the entrance to Pendynas (Pendennis) Castle which is a promontory fortification several thousands of years in age with a "modern" 16th century castle erected by the Killigrew and Arundel families, the Bailiffs using their usual modus operandi (oxy acetylene cutting equipment), cut through the legs of a large English Heritage sign, placed it upon their roof rack and proceeded to sign number 2. With "The Conquest of America" by ~Van Gellis, a piece of music played at the recent funeral of Stannator W.D. Nute being played at full bore on the car cassette player and in view of curious visitors, the hissing gas axe removed the second sign (all signs were removed between the working hours of 8am and 5pm and in full view of the public). Proceeding around to the seaward entrance to Pendynas Castle, a 3rd sign was spotted adjacent to the entrance.

The car was parked, the gas bottles unloaded and the last of the offensive signs at Pendynas Castle met its just fate. While the Bailiff cut through the sign's legs with the sign being held by the Assistant Bailiff, the Bailiff heard running footsteps approaching and an English voice saying, "what the hell are you doing?" The reply from the Assistant Bailiff was "preventing the theft of our heritage". The footsteps retreated back into the castle. The Bailiffs loaded the third sign onto the roof rack, they then sat down, rolled a smoke and discussed the situation. As there were only two more signs left to be confiscated in the whole of Cornwall and as the Police appeared reluctant to be involved but surely would attend now that the Official at Pendynas Castle must have called them, it was decided to wait awhile as being arrested would bring the matter to court for resolution. After a considerable period of waiting the Bailiffs decided to rearrange the loading of the signs on the roof rack. This being done and still no sign of the Police, it was decided to leave and proceed very slowly down the road. At a crawl the Bailiffs' car approached Gyllyngvase Beach, two Police cars raced by going in the direction of Pendynas Castle. Continuing slowly with an eye in the mirror, sure enough the two Police cars reappeared racing back down the road. The Bailiff indicated left and pulled into the side of the road and parked. The Police cars then switched on their flashing lights and sirens and with one car stopping close up behind and the other slewed across the Bailiffs' bow, it was 'captured NYPD style'. After an amusing conversation the Police officers decided that the Bailiffs were to be taken to Camborne Police Station in a Police van. Upon arriving at the Police station, the Bailiffs discovered that the Stannary photographer had also been arrested.

After giving their names and addresses and having been measured, DNA tested, their belts and shoe laces taken, the two Bailiffs and photographer were taken to the cells, having not yet been charged. After spending around 10½ hours there, during which time they were individually interviewed (taped) then released to reappear there the following Saturday to be charged. After being charged with theft, all three attended some seven preliminary court hearings before appearing at the Crown Court in Truro.

Presiding at what was supposedly a 'criminal trial' was Judge Rucker. The jury seats were and remained empty. The proceedings began with the three defendants being seated in an alcove at the back of the courtroom as far from the Judge as it was possible to be with a glass panel between them and the Judge.

The court clerk rose and appeared to be speaking to the Bailiff who, being at the far end of the room and behind a glass panel, could not properly hear the words spoken by the clerk so he nodded to the clerk expecting a repeat. The clerk then appeared to speak to the Assistant Bailiff and then the photographer, neither could properly hear the faint voice due to the ridiculous configuration of the court room so neither answered. Upon this Judge Rucker like some purple-faced potentate delivering a death sentence, shouted "I'll not have these shenanigans in my court, these men are guilty. There is no excuse for theft I want this case brought before me" and so on. The Honourable Judge had condemned the defendants out of hand before hearing any evidence from either side.

The defendants' Barristers were so shocked by the Judge's outburst that they gathered statements from persons in the courtroom and caused Judge Rucker to dismiss himself from any further involvement in the case due to his biased and narrow-minded attitude.

Two weeks before the next "trial", the Crown Prosecution Service made an emergency application to the trial Judge for a 'Public Interest and Immunity Certificate'.

A Public Interest and Immunity Certificate (PII) has since been deemed "incompatible" by the European Court of Human Rights.

Dear Sirs   27th December 2001

ELIZABETH REGINA v NUTE, ROWE & HICKS

I write to advise you that an application relating to disclosure is to be made before the trial Judge. The application relates to sensitive material and the prosection is not able to give any indication of the category of the material.

T, Jones
Crown Court Unit

This meant that in the 'public interest' certain evidence could be banned from inclusion in a trial and that 'immunity' (in this case immunity for the Duke of Cornwall) supposedly involving threats to national security, the national interest and defence of the realm would prevent the accused from bringing forth Charters or Acts of Parliament involving the Duke or the Duchy in evidence for their defence. With regard to the use of Public Interest and Immunity Certificates, *"preventing the defendant from having access to secret documents but giving them to the Judge is a fundamental erosion of the right to a fair trial"* – (John Wadham Director of civil rights group "Liberty"). As much of the defendants' case was based upon such Charters and Acts of Parliament, the accused had therefore been denied the use of the very principle tenets of law in their defence.

Inexplicably all three Barristers representing the defendants were suddenly unable to attend the forthcoming trial. The accused were left with no Barristers and a watertight case against the <u>Crown</u> that had been vandalised by a Public Interest and <u>Immunity</u> Certificate. With great difficulty another Barrister was found just before the forthcoming trial. This Barrister had no time to familiarise himself with such a complicated and potentially emasculated defence case.

The day of the trial arrived, presiding was Judge Cottle. The defendants were no longer facing a charge of theft but now faced a much more serious charge of conspiracy with a potential sentence of 10 years imprisonment. The charge of conspiracy had been brought against the defendants by the **Crown** Prosecution Service for resolution in a **Crown** Court presided over by a **Crown** <u>Judge</u>. Their excellent case against the **Crown** had been torpedoed by a **Crown** Public Interest and Immunity Certificate and also their own Barrister had sworn allegiance to the **Crown** in the case of "**Elizabeth Regina** -v- Nute, Rowe and Hicks".

Having already been declared guilty by Judge Rucker at the commencement of the previous 'non-trial', would the three defendants emerge alive from this great temple to justice?

The trial began with the usual preliminaries, then the **Crown** prosecution Barrister said quietly to the **Crown** Judge that he wanted a private word to discuss something. They left the Court together for a secret discussion.

Upon their return, there was an adjournment, the defendants' Barrister who had not been privy to the secret discussion did not know why there was an adjournment and was asked by the defendants to find out what was going on. Upon his return it transpired that the **Crown** Prosecution Service wanted an out of court agreement. Their terms were, that if the defendants paid £20,000 in damages to the signs, returned the signs and be bound over to keep the peace, then they would drop all charges.

The defendants discussed the terms between themselves. They realised that their excellent defence case had been circumvented in a typically feudal manner and that due to this they would certainly receive a jail sentence of up to 10 years, plus court costs which could easily exceed £200,000. They sent their Barrister with their reply which was £450 for damage to the signs (as unavoidably the tax payer had been caused expense), the signs returned, provided they were never again erected in Cornwall and, as for being bound over to keep the peace, then that was no problem as they had never broken the peace. The Barrister returned with the message that the defendants' terms were agreeable.

Returning to the courtroom the deal was done, the defendants bound over to keep the peace and the Judge gave the defendants a **NOT GUILTY VERDICT.**

A clerk of the **Crown** Court then went to the press reporters present and issued them with a paper saying, "this is what you **will** print" (there are witnesses to this). The press then printed that the defendants were found guilty and fined, neither of which was true.

It was later noticed by the defendants that in the agreement they had signed, the £450 had grown to £4,500.

Under Contract Law it is illegal to enter into an agreement which stifles a prosecution (English Law)

In a criminal case of a man accused of burglary, would the prosecution Barrister be able to expect the Judge to give consent to an agreement whereby all charges be dropped if the defendant gave to the victim a wad of cash?

Observation

As Cornwall was excluded from the union between England, Wales and Scotland due to its separate constitutional status and therefore not included in the UK, then it must follow that the Queen of the UK (who represents the Crown in England) but who has no authority in Cornwall which is constitutionally a possession of the Duke, should not be able to bring cases against Cornish people as in "Elizabeth Regina –v- Nute, Rowe and Hicks". This should constitutionally be the "Duke of Cornwall -v- Nute, Rowe and Hicks".

Why was a Public Interest and Immunity Certificate served on the defendants? This is only usually used in extreme cases i.e. where defence of the Realm is deemed necessary. Was it because the defendants' case was unbeatable by any other means, was it to protect the Duke from having his dirty washing aired in public or was it to prevent the peoples of Britain from learning of the true constitutional position of Cornwall as a national entity in its own right?

Why did the **Crown** Prosecution Service and Judge Cottel allow an out of court agreement instead of a legal contest between the defenders of Cornish Heritage and the **Crown**? **Under Contract Law it is illegal to enter into an agreement which stifles a prosecution (English Law)**

Many years ago there existed a Cornish Press that was not afraid to criticise government policy. Now we are lumbered with an English controlled press, radio and television that obey their masters in another land.

Truro Crown Court

FREEDOM TO FLY THE FLAG

In April 1995, District Councils in Cornwall were under pressure from central government to demand planning permission and a fee of £45.00 from anyone wanting to fly the Cornish flag. The Constitutional Committee of the Cornish Stannary Parliament persuaded a potential victim of this policy who had already complained unsuccessfully to the Council, that the Stannary could help.

The Cornish Stannary Parliament passed a resolution rejecting the Council's action and giving 'Cornish people the freedom to fly the flag of St. Piran'. The Council was notified and the original complainant advised to raise her flag. Over 12 months later the flag was still flying and no contact had been made by the council. Many other Cornish people now feel free to fly the Cornish national flag.

Some time ago a young man called Marcus decided that it would be a good idea to sell car number plates with a Cornish flag depicted on the left side. These proved to be very popular and soon others started to sell them as well until many cars were proudly displaying them. A Ministry of Transport Enforcement Officer who was checking vehicles at Blackwater, told drivers with these plates fitted that they were illegal and must be removed at once. He then contacted Marcus and requested a list of all vehicles which he had supplied with these so called illegal plates but Marcus, a true Cornishman, refused in no uncertain terms. The M.O.T. Officer then promised to take legal action upon his return to his head office to which Marcus replied "please do" but no legal action was ever taken and Marcus heard no more about the matter.

Could this have been another example of the powers that be not wanting to raise 'THE CORNISH QUESTION'?

CULTURAL DIVERSITY

In advance of the official 2001 and 2011 census the Cornish Stannary Parliament made representations to the Census Office with a detailed case of the Cornish national identity with reference to prescriptive rights and The Framework Convention for the Protection of National Minorities. The only method of achieving a true record of people of Cornish nationality is to correctly entitle the census form 'Census Cornwall'. In the 1991 census entitled 'Census England', one Cornishman obviously not English and residing in Cornwall and not in England, found himself unable to complete a census form entitled 'Census England. He was charged with neglecting to complete a census form and after appearing in court for the third time, the Department of Public Prosecutions dropped the charge against him.

The Census Act states that there shall be a census taken for 'BRITAIN'. If the Office for National Statistics wishes to divide Britain into its constituent parts then there must be separate census forms for Cornwall, England, Scotland and Wales.

The same Cornishman has not completed an 'England Census' for more than 30 years. He was again unable to complete the 2011 census form that was unfortunately entitled 'ENGLAND HOUSEHOLD'.

A large number of Cornish people have also found themselves unable to complete such an assimilative form even when threatened with a £1000 fine or imprisonment. The Office for National Statistics appears unable to comply with human rights including their own Human Rights Act.

Could it be that there is a reluctance by the English authorities to have "the Cornish question" raised in a Court of law for fear of the truth coming out. Further Stannary contact is in progress to establish Cornwall as a separate European Region.

The end of Empire as in the case of the break up of the Soviet Union gives rebirth to nations that few people had ever heard of such as Moldavia, Kazakhstan and Azerbaijan. The world including the British will want information about these nations and hopefully press for their right to maintain their independence.

Is it possible that with an institutionalised policy of assimilation, assisted by an imposed monarchical monoculture, that the principle of cultural diversity in Cornwall is being denied by those who foolishly believe that England is an island and that Englishness is something that Cornish people should aspire to?

THE CAMBORNE SCHOOL OF MINES

Since it was established in 1876 by a Cornish benefactor, the world renowned Camborne School of Mines has built a reputation as the leading world authority on mining. Former students in countries around the world have established over 35 associations and created what has in effect become a 'Camborne School of Mines International'.

This year on the weekend of the 31st March 2012 Cornwall is to host at South Condurrow Mine, Troon, Camborne the International Mining Students Games. This will be the 34th year that the games have been held internationally and for the first time in Britain.

Cornish people were anxious to ensure that this Cornish mining establishment retained its world-renowned signature of quality 'The Camborne School of Mines' and remained in Cornwall to enhance the status of a new University of Cornwall.

Instead the long tentacle of assimilation has reached down from the 'English' University of Exeter in an attempt to falsely portray the Camborne School of Mines as an English entity.

MINERALS PLAN

The Stannary Parliament submitted a report to the then Cornwall (County) Council in respect of future land reclamation and mineral extraction plans in Cornwall; the main points of which were:-

1. Land reclamation represents a shortsighted destruction of valuable assets. The over 200 engine houses, mining and geological sites of Cornwall should

form the basis of an expanding cultural heritage trail for cultural tourism and a geological education policy.

2. More research is required into job creation through the use of indigenous mineral resources, such as china clay which is currently exported as a raw material.

THE CELTIC COUNTRY OF THE WEST

After much effort between February and July 1996, the Cornish Stannary Parliament persuaded the European Commission in London that it should reprint its booklet 'The South West' first published in February 1996. The booklet deliberately excluded Cornwall by ignoring official Cornish submissions to the editors. The Stannary Parliament felt obliged to accuse the Commission in London of calculated racial discrimination. It was also argued that Cornwall is a Celtic region of Europe and this fact is widely known. The European Commission in London subsequently agreed to reprint this booklet.

We gratefully acknowledged the support given by Alastair Quinnell, who was at the time Chairman of the then Cornwall (County) Council's European Committee, in our struggle to prevent this abuse of power in trying to incorporate the Cornish nation into a South West region of England.

Cornwall although the oldest nation of Britain is being discriminated against by being incorporated with 'The South West' or 'The West Country' and overall being assimilated into England without its consent.

The Cornish Stannary Parliament requires that the British government recognises Cornwall's right to continue its international role as one of the four nations of Britain.

CORNISH MINING - WORD HERITAGE

The United Nations Educational, Scientific and Cultural Organisation (UNESCO) accepted Cornish Mining and Culture as World Heritage, based on the Nomination Bid Document submitted to UNESCO by the U.K.

The Cornish Stannary Parliament ensured that previous deliberations considered the UNESCO NARA Document on Authenticity.

"The search for cultural identity is sometimes pursued through aggressive nationalism and the suppression of the cultures of minorities" (NARA document).

Extracts from the "World Heritage Site Management Plan (2005 - 2010)

"World Heritage Sites are inscribed by UNESCO for their "outstanding universal value….." the cultural tradition of non-ferrous hard rock mining that contributed to the development of the Industrial Revolution in Britain and pioneered its transfer overseas….. In recognition of this unique contribution to the development of the modern industrialised world"

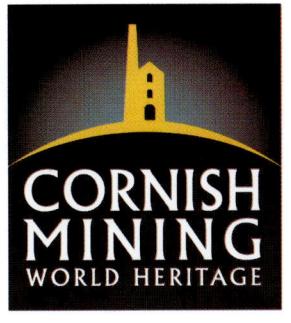

"Cornwall…contained Europe's principal tin deposits and satisfied substantial demand over four millennia"

"Cornwall was locked into the global economy at an early stage. As a leader in mining expertise its miners were in demand in other, newer mining regions. By the 1820's Cornish miners were being recruited for mines in Latin America. Within a generation a flourishing culture of emigration had been created and links with North America and Australia forged. During the fall in world copper prices in the late 1860's and the crisis decade of the 1870's, when tin prices were also in recession, the Cornish had a ready made option. They left. Indeed, Cornwall became one of Europe's major emigration regions with perhaps 200,000 people leaving in the century after 1830"

Such was the expertise of the Cornish miner that the Moonta mine in Southern Australia employed around 8000 people, from top management down – all Cornish.

It must be understood that Cornwall has four millennia of history, tradition and culture in metalliferous mining and that more than half that period occurred before the arrival of the Anglo Saxon (proto English) people in the island of Britain.

As the Cornish are indigenous people and occupying their own territory for at least the past 17,000 years, then to consider that English Heritage has any credence to the west of the River Tamar is a nonsense.

The Ayatollahs of assimilation continue to promote English Heritage within Cornwall, and some more gullible Cornish people are prepared to work with them - a case of seeking guidance from the misguided.

AN GOF COMMEMORATION – 500th ANNIVERSARY

1997 was the year of commemorating the struggle of "An Gof" and his followers to assert the rights of the Cornish people in 1497. A tax levy was imposed on Cornwall so that it would finance an English invasion of Scotland by King Henry VII. A blacksmith from St. Keverne called Michael Joseph spoke out against the subsidy which would penalise the poor people of Cornwall. Thomas Flamank was a lawyer from Bodmin and was joined by Michael Joseph and together with other leaders and their followers who joined them on their way through Cornwall, and the West of England, marched to Blackheath in London with 15,000 men to protest. Before being attacked a large number of the followers had left. The remaining men were overcome at Blackheath by Henry's army of 25,000 who had been assembled to attack Scotland but were instead turned upon the Cornish. The leaders were brought to London in chains where they were sentenced to death, as were many others, and were hanged, drawn and quartered. It is estimated that over 2000 Cornishmen are buried in a mass grave at Blackheath.

Thomas Flamank - Mighal Joseph

A statue to Michael Joseph ("An Gof" - the Smith) and Thomas Flamank (Lawyer) was unveiled in St. Keverne in 1997. This was the year for the march from St. Keverne to Blackheath. It was a year of historical commemoration but also a year to promote Cornwall and celebrate the many surviving aspects of Cornish cultural diversity as well as a time to look to the future and encourage young people to develop a positive view of Cornishness. It was decided to call the event Keskerdh Kernow (Cornwall Marches On) in order to promote the idea of an actively forward looking Cornwall marching into the next millennium.

The march was from St. Keverne to Blackheath and took 30 days. 1,600 became day walkers but 37 people went the whole distance carrying flags, banners and some wearing Cornish kilts. The Blackheath Declaration was signed by all those present containing proposals that would lead to the economic betterment of Cornwall and give self respect to local people through support for Cornwall's distinct identity and heritage.

From 1st January 1997 in honour of the sacrifices made by An Gof and his followers, the Cornish Stannary Parliament will consider proposals to veto all statutes and acts or proclamations from whatever source which are in contravention of 'The Framework Convention for the Protection of National Minorities.

"I shall have a name perpetual and a fame permanent and immortal."
These were the words of Michael Joseph An Gof, the legendary blacksmith of St. Keverne on his way through the streets of London in 1497 before his execution at Tyburne.

These words were well chosen because more than 500 years later he is still remembered and revered and is commemorated annually in his birthplace on the 27th June, whilst his great valour and courage are increasingly an inspiration to Cornish people both at home and overseas.

This informative book enables the An Gof spirit to continue. (A Richards)

CORNWALL AND THE FUTURE

What action can be taken to change the experiences of the past? Cornwall is still a low wage economy with too many people forced to migrate in search of better opportunities. Families become divided and the quality of life suffers. Many Cornish jobs have been exported to England such as the ambulance service, police service, water, electric and gas services whereas top jobs in local government, central government and education are advertised to 'attract' people from England for example by diverting many millions of EU funding designated for Cornwall to English administration and projects. We are told that these people are experienced as if they had gained experience by first working in America or Germany. Are we expected to believe that only the English are experienced? Teachers with English regional dialects arrive and incline to forbid or ridicule the Cornish accent. What sort of "experience" is that?

The Cornish accent derives from the ancient indigenous Cornish language whereas the English regional dialects derive from the Germanic languages of the proto English tribes.

To deny a people their accent and to further impose some foreign dialect upon them through a state sponsored assimilative educational system is, apart from being a despicable act, contrary to universal human rights laws.

In elections to the House of Commons, Cornwall was only allocated a maximum of six members out of a total of 650. Even with the help of all Scottish and Welsh MP's, it would still only be 6+72+36 making a total of 114. This potential group of Celtic MP's represents 18% of the House of Commons which is nowhere near enough to out-vote the imposition of English bias into the Celtic lands. Local government in Cornwall is secretly run by unpublished directives from the many Government Offices who operate without principles. The public and councillors are too often dictated to regarding decisions without consultation. Political parties receive donations from overseas benefactors to pay for the advertising that will probably determine the result of the next election.

Cornish taxes must be used to promote Cornish traditions, Cornish education, Cornish heritage and investment in jobs for people in Cornwall.

In line with the European movement towards regional self-government from Saxony in Germany to Catalonia in Spain, the regions are asserting their own identity and making themselves felt in policy decisions of the European Union.

Cornwall has historic and contemporary credentials to push for full recognition as a region of Europe. Obviously international rules across Europe should apply to everyone so that life in the regions is not distorted by policies designed for urban areas being imposed upon the regions. Working with other regions in Europe who share Cornwall's problems, Cornwall can influence and control over centralised bureaucratic interference whether from Brussels, London, Bristol, Exeter or Plymouth.

Despite protest Cornwall's office in Brussels has since been arbitrarily axed.

With tourism here to stay, every region is making the most of available resources. Cornwall has irreplaceable Celtic assets which can become the motor for its future. With fishing and farming under threat, Cornwall will sorely need its World Heritage mining sites to promote cultural tourism as the backbone of its economy while attracting investments for example to promote Cornish china clay as a manufacturing raw material in Cornwall for the people of Cornwall.

Cornish destiny must lie in Cornish hands

It is acknowledged that if Cornwall were treated as a separate unit by withdrawing from the South West Region with Devon, Cornwall would qualify for a much higher level of grants from Europe, particularly without the Westminster administration charges.

The European Commissioner for Regional Policy has written to the Cornish Stannary Parliament stating that she supports Cornwall's Celtic culture and heritage. The Commissioner concludes: "**We hope that the Stannary Parliament will be able to play its full role in this**". (Regional Policy)

Unfortunately the Stannary Parliament has been prevented from fulfilling this

MP Andrew George on 3rd December 2011 stated that "we have been discriminated against under "The Race Relations Act" which the Westminster government still refuses to acknowledge..... there has been a very limp response from Westminster" (re the Framework Convention for the Protection of National Minorities)

The way forward requires this level of confidence in Cornwall's Celtic identity. This is the basis on which to insist on the rights of the Cornish as an indigenous national minority under the Framework Convention for the Protection of National Minorities signed by the British government on 1st February 1995.

As yet the elder of the British nations (the Cornish) has been prevented from inclusion in to the Framework Convention for the protection of National Minorities by the British government.

"States are obliged to give effect to the obligations they have assumed under any treaty to which they are a party in accordance with the provisions of international law." - Foreign and Commonwealth Office, Human Rights Policy Department 15 April 1996.

This international convention prohibits any measure (Article 16) which "alters the proportion of the population in areas inhabited by persons belonging to a national minority".

Since the 1950's the population of Cornwall has gone from virtually completely Cornish to around 50% Cornish, this coupled with an imposed English educational system which busies itself by teaching Cornish children that they are English (changing Celt into Saxon) and grubbing out the Cornish accent, can only be described as deliberate assimilation particularly as there is no provision by way of a Cornish national census form to allow Cornish people their right of "freedom of expression" in declaring themselves factually to be members of the Cornish nation.

The Cornish qualify as a nation according to international standards on a number of grounds but specifically as a result of the documentary evidence from many Cornish organisations which led the European Parliament to recognise the Celtic identity of Cornwall, its language, culture and traditions.

Some well meaning Cornish organisations have suggested 'an Assembly for Cornwall' as a temporary solution, apparently without considering the implications. Translated into practice, a Cornish Assembly given by Westminster would mean nothing more than giving the present Cornwall Council a new name. Control over policies would still lie with existing English political parties and their bureaucrats. A Cornish Assembly would in more ways than one, represent a blind alley and a surrender of potential and status.

"Power devolved is power retained" Enoch Powell

Such well meaning Cornish organisations do not seem to realise that any "Assembly" gained from Westminster would in fact be an **English** regional assembly. Cornwall is not a region of England. If Cornwall were to be wrongly recognised as such then the Cornish would have to recognise themselves as being an ethnic group within England. This would automatically disbar them from their true status as a national minority of Britain, subsequently rendering inclusion into the Framework Convention for the protection of National Minorities impossible.

The future government of Cornwall must be based on the prescriptive and constitutional rights of the Cornish people to their own recognised and legitimate Parliament which has never been surrendered.

CONCLUSION

The Cornish have contributed to the spread of ideas, the development of technologies and social change to the evolution of democracy, of science and the arts and have helped to build great societies such as America and Australia. That contribution continues as the challenge of climate change, the opportunities of new technologies, creativity and space exploration harness the talents of this enquiring, creative and spiritually energetic people. (Cornish National Minority Report by Cornwall Council 2011).

The Cornish have inhabited their own territory for at least 17,000 years and are by far the oldest industrial nation of Britain of some 4,000 years standing. For some 1,500 years they have resisted and continue to resist domination by the neighbouring Anglo-Saxon people.

Tacitus, a Roman in the first century A.D, described the Britons thus: "..... they can bear the tribute and conscription, provided always that there is no injustice, for this they take very ill, for they will be the slaves of no man"

"The early inhabitants of Cornwall were of Celtic origin. The Anglo Saxon settlement of England did not extend to their territory and the people of Cornwall continued to be Celtic. (Royal Commission on the Constitution 1973)

The Cornish parliament originating in times B.C. and continuous (except for two periods of oppression) and convening regularly to the present day, would appear to be the longest existing parliament on earth.

The latest genetic studies of the peoples of Britain indicate that the Cornish are the elder of the truly indigenous peoples of this island whose language originates from the very first people to inhabit Britain.

Far from being described as the fourth nation of Britain, the Cornish are in fact the first nation of Britain.

It is those ethnic Anglo-Saxons whose origins do not stem from this island who wilfully obstruct Cornwall's entry into the Framework Convention for the Protection of National Minorities, who are insulting the intelligence of the Cornish, the other Celtic nations of Britain and the peoples of Europe whose compassion for the smaller nations, led to the creation of the Framework Convention.

Although some of us may not live to see, it will be of great interest to the reader to follow subsequent events in this 21st century of land grabs, oil grabs, the effects of climate change, such as water grabs, extreme weather effects upon populations with subsequent assimilations and possible genocides, probably wars over both the Arctic and Antarctic, all effected by the corruptibility of mankind.

As for the Cornish, they will remain as a fact to be the first nation of the island of Britain regardless of any world catastrophe as long as one of them survives.